ISBN 978-1-331-08725-0
PIBN 10143119

1 MONTH OF
FREE
READING

at

www.ForgottenBooks.com

By purchasing this book you are eligible for one month membership to ForgottenBooks.com, giving you unlimited access to our entire collection of over 700,000 titles via our web site and mobile apps.

To claim your free month visit:

www.forgottenbooks.com/free143119

English
Français
Deutsche
Italiano
Español
Português

www.forgottenbooks.com

Mythology Photography **Fiction**
Fishing Christianity **Art** Cooking
Essays Buddhism Freemasonry
Medicine **Biology** Music **Ancient
Egypt** Evolution Carpentry Physics
Dance Geology **Mathematics** Fitness
Shakespeare **Folklore** Yoga Marketing
Confidence Immortality Biographies
Poetry **Psychology** Witchcraft
Electronics Chemistry History **Law**
Accounting **Philosophy** Anthropology
Alchemy Drama Quantum Mechanics
Atheism Sexual Health **Ancient History**
Entrepreneurship Languages Sport
Paleontology Needlework Islam
Metaphysics Investment Archaeology
Parenting Statistics Criminology
Motivational

SAINT JOHN BAPTIST DE LA SALLE
1651-1719

The Story of
St. John Baptist de la Salle

FOUNDER OF THE INSTITUTE OF
THE BROTHERS OF THE CHRISTIAN SCHOOLS

BY

BROTHER LEO

INTRODUCTION BY

MOST REV. PATRICK J. HAYES, D.D.
ARCHBISHOP OF NEW YORK

NEW YORK
P. J. KENEDY & SONS
PUBLISHERS TO THE HOLY APOSTOLIC SEE
1921

Nibil Obstat:

ARTHURUS J. SCANLAN, S.T.D.
Censor Librorum

Imprimatur

✠ PATRITIUS J. HAYES, D.D.
Archiepiscopus Neo-Eboracensis

Neo-Eboraci
die, 13 Aprilis, 1921

INTRODUCTION

THIS well-told story of St. John Baptist de la Salle is refreshing, intellectually and spiritually, coming, as it does, at a time when education is drifting steadily far away from its highest and holiest purpose, namely, the knowledge and love of God. Through the existing maze of false principle and unsound method in pedagogy, it should prove helpful to read and study the life of a Teacher Saint like that of the canonized Founder of the Brothers of the Christian Schools.

Today, popular education, put by the State within the reach of all, is hailed as an accepted standard of modern progress and a pledge of civic liberty and of social welfare. If this be so, then our Saint was far in advance of his day and should be heralded a benefactor of the plain people, because of the entire consecration of himself to the training, religious and secular, of their children.

St. John Baptist de la Salle did for the common school system among the people what St. Vincent de Paul wrought for the social betterment of the masses. The God-given birthright of the children of men, that is, the right and privilege of heavenly citizenship rather than the urge of social democracy, inspired these Saints of God to labor with zeal and success extraordinary among the wage-earners of their day,

Our Saint made it possible for the sons of the toiler on farm and in shop to enjoy the opportunities of elementary, higher and technical schools—a blessing reserved generally to the children of the well-to-do. The course of study embraced the common branches of secular education together with a solid training in religious knowledge and piety. The complete thoroughness and soundness of the method turned out youth that was reverent towards God, dutiful to parents, and fitted for a useful life in the community.

This was a revolutionary change in the school world in favor of the working classes. It will be the better understood, if we remember that our ideals and practices of democracy did not then obtain; in fact, they were not known to the people. Rigid social and class distinction was the recognized custom, if not the law of the land. St. John Baptist de la Salle was of the aristocracy. Though close to the royal court, he knew that the *élite* of France was not necessarily the *élite* of Christ. He knew also that the peasant and artisan, in the humble walks of life, could never move in the circle of royalty. Nor did he lament this privation. For he knew further that there was a king—Christ the Lord, and a queen—Mary Immaculate, and princes—the Angels and the Saints, to whom the children of the plough and of the hammer should be suffered to come that they might enter the banquet hall of the Eucharistic Lord and move in the courts of the God of Infinite love. To accomplish this was the mission of the Saint.

The extraordinary success our Saint achieved before his death has been carried on by the Religious Institute he founded, whose members are committed to the teaching of youth the world over, with a consecration that is as rare as it is inspiring, because of the spirit of faith and humility, of prayer and study that animates their own lives while they are moulding the character of others.

This little volume is most readable and instructive. The author's keen insight into the times of St. John Baptist de la Salle and the clear style that brightens nearly every page with quaint and modern phrase or with homely parable, should make the reading attractive to teachers and pupils, and to educators generally, who would know wherein is hidden the secret of true education.

✝ PATRICK J. HAYES,
Archbishop of New York.

CONTENTS

The Story of
St. John Baptist de la Salle

CHAPTER I

A KING AND A SAINT

"My brethren, God alone is great."

THOSE WERE the opening words of one of the greatest funeral sermons ever preached. It was a great sermon, because the preacher was a famous orator, Father Massillon; and because the words were uttered over the mortal remains of one of earth's greatest kings. That king was Louis XIV, who had ruled for half a century over France, the king whom historians have called the Great King (le Grand Monarque) and whose power was recognized at home and abroad. It was a great sermon, too, because many of the great ones of the earth were there to listen to it—kings and queens and ambassadors, generals and admirals and statesmen—wearing costly mourning garments and flanked by numerous attendants. And the first words of that sermon are its greatest words, because they contain the deepest and most impressive truth.

That was more than two hundred years ago, in September, 1715. And four years later another man died. He was not a king, and the greatest preacher in France did not speak at his funeral. He died, not in a gorgeous palace, but in a plain, ill-lighted room; and the great ones of the earth did not come to follow his body to the grave. His remains were borne on the shoulders of men wearing the black habit of the Christian Brother; and along the streets the people—the plain people, the common people, the poor people—gathered with tears in their eyes and on their lips the words: "The saint is dead! The saint is dead!" That man was St. John Baptist de la Salle, the priest who founded the Institute of the Christian Schools.

Those two men—the king and the saint—who died about the same time, at the beginning of the eighteenth century—were about as different in their lives and in their deaths as two men could well be. And in the eyes of the world—the world which looked only on the outside of things and was much impressed by pomp and glare—there could be no comparison between them. Louis XIV had feasted delicately and had gone about clad in magnificent attire and had waged mighty wars and had been surrounded by fawning courtiers and flatterers; St. de la Salle had eaten only the plainest food and had worn the humble priest's soutane, he had fought no enemies but sin and ignorance, and had been attended only by a few simple, holy men—

the first Christian Brothers. To the eyes of the world Louis XIV was truly the Great King, and St. de la Salle was just a simple, zealous priest.

In the eyes of God those two men were very different, too; but the difference was all the other way. For Louis XIV, though he had been careful about enhancing the glory of his kingdom, had been careless about saving his own soul; he had not been a good king like his great and holy predecessor, St. Louis, King Louis IX. The Great King had been a very selfish man, and had used his high place in life as a means of securing his own pleasure at the expense of his subjects; the country had been heavily taxed in order that no whim of his might be denied, and many Frenchmen gave their lives in wars that served only to add to the glory of the king. But, on the other hand, St. de la Salle lived his life in the belief that the soul is the only part of a man that really matters, that not all the kingdoms of the world and the glory of them are of any worth in comparison with one immortal soul. And so he had given away all that he possessed in order to labor for the salvation of souls, especially the souls of boys; and the army he organized and led into battle was not an army bent on conquest or on earthly fame, but an army of Christian teachers, destined to carry the flag of Christ and His Church throughout France and throughout all the world, bringing light to darkened minds and grace to sin-stained souls.

In our day, even the world, looking at those two men, must doubt if the Great King was really as great as his admirers supposed; must conclude, indeed, that the humble priest who sought to bring faith and liberty to the minds of the young was far the greater man.   There is a famous saying that has often been attributed to Louis XIV: "I am the state."   What did it mean?   It meant that the king's word was law, that the king could do no wrong, that the king was the entire government of the people. "It is God's will," the Great King wrote in his memoirs, "that every one born a subject should obey the King without question "   And less than a hundred years after the Great King's death came the terrible French Revolution, in which the people of the land rose up against the successors of Louis XIV and destroyed everything that the Great King had most esteemed.   Where now were his military conquests and his fine garments and his lavish entertainments in the gardens at Versailles?   The work of his hand had come to naught.

But it was otherwise with the work of St. de la Salle.   That work, though little noticed in the time of Louis XIV, has grown and grown until it is recognized everywhere as one of the best and biggest things in all the world.   In the very year when King Louis was questioning the right of Our Holy Father, the Pope, to decide on Church affairs in France, St. de la Salle was laying the foundations of his Institute of the Christian Schools, a body of teachers destined to spread loyalty to the Church and to the Pope in every Christian land.

Louis XIV was one of the richest of men and the richest of kings.   Filled with vainglory and foolish ambition, he spent nearly two hundred million francs (forty millions of dollars in our money) trying to build an aqueduct from the River Eure to his palace at Versailles. He wished to leave behind him something to rival the famous aqueducts of ancient Rome. The Louvre in Paris was not palace enough for the Great King, so he constructed at Versailles a dwelling place that cost some five hundred million francs—money that had to come from his oppressed subjects. In such ways the Great Monarch delighted to squander vast sums, while many of his people lacked enough food to keep them alive.

St. de la Salle was one of the poorest of men and the poorest of priests. He came of a noble and wealthy family, but he freely gave away his inheritance to the poor of his native city; and in time of famine—and there were several famines during the reign of the Great King—he tasted the bitter pangs of want. Far from seeking a stylish place to live in, he gave up his fine family residence and went to live with the poor men who were the first Brothers; and he always chose the smallest and darkest room in the house. He had no thought of rivalling the deeds of the ancient Romans or of anybody else; his great object, his sole object, was to become more and more like Our Blessed Lord, Who was born in a cold stable and who through all His life had not whereon to lay His head.

In the days when kings and queens ruled in the world and were much more plentiful than they are now, they often received credit for fine things and great things and good things with which they usually had little or nothing to do. Thus, Queen Elizabeth of England got almost all the glory of the defeat of the Spanish Armada, while in fact the victory was due to a storm which dispersed the Spanish ships. And so it was that Louis XIV won renown—and gave his name to a period in history—mainly because there arose during his reign famous captains and writers and statesmen and saints. The Great King did not have to build a kingdom or to establish a government; that work had been done in France before his time by great kings like Henry IV and great statesmen like Cardinal Richelieu.

But it was very different with the work undertaken by St. de la Salle. He had to begin at the beginning. He had to find schools and teachers; and he had to interest wealthy people in the work in order that the schools might continue and the teachers might not starve. He had to overcome the opposition that always arises in this world when a great man attempts to do something unusual, especially if it is something good. He had to teach the teachers—a most important part of his work and something that until then had been almost entirely neglected. He had to write textbooks and organize free libraries and superintend Sunday schools and establish technical institutes and boarding colleges. And the bulk of this work he had to do quite by himself; he had no capable and willing statesmen, as the Great King had, to do the work for him. And so St. de la Salle did the work, and did it all, and did it well; and he gave the glory of it to Almighty God.

Even before his death the alleged greatness of King Louis XIV had begun to crumble and crack; not without reason might he murmur: "After me, the Deluge!" In his declining years the Great King saw his once powerful army routed by the Duke of Marlborough at Blenheim and Ramillies; and in the Peace of Utrecht, in 1713, he was obliged to cede to England many of France's American possessions, including Acadia, the land of Longfellow's "Evangeline." Before his death he expressed regret for his pride and ambition which had brought affliction and misery to so many of his subjects, and with contrition he confessed his more personal sins. Let us hope that God, who is infinitely merciful, granted His plenteous forgiveness to that repentant old man of seventy-seven—the Great King trembling in the presence of Death, a greater king than he.

But King Death had no terrors for St. de la Salle. To die meant for him but to go into the presence of his God whom he had loved so much and served so faithfully through sixty-eight years of life. His last days were cheered by the progress of the schools he had founded throughout France, by the growth in numbers and in holiness of the Brothers he had gathered together to teach the neglected boys and young men of town and country. He could leave this world eagerly, happily, as the saints always do, knowing that God had blessed his work and would preserve it and make it grow. His favorite motto was not, "I am the state"; it was the little prayer that to this day the pupils of the Brothers use when responding to roll call, "God be blessed!" And his last words were these: "I adore in all things the will of God in my regard."

And so, of those two men who died in France two hundred years ago and more, it would seem that to-day the humble saint, and not the worldly king, is the greater hero and the greater man. Anyway, to be a saint is better than to be a king; for we could get along quite well without any kings at all, but we cannot get along without saints. There are always saints in the world, though often they are not thought to be saints; indeed, perhaps the greatest saints of all are the hidden saints whose holiness is known only to God.

Now, this little book will help us to understand what a saint really is by telling us a few things about one. Already we are able to see that the Great King was not a saint and that the founder of the Brothers was a saint. And what was the essential difference between them? It was just this: That St. John Baptist de la Salle realized every day and every hour the truth of Father Massillon's words, "God alone is great," while Louis XIV did not realize it until he lay on his death-bed.

CHAPTER II
A PICTURE OF THE AGE

IF we are to understand rightly the life of a great man, we must know something of the age in which he lived. To evaluate the military genius of Hannibal we must have some conception of the geographical relations of Spain, Northern Africa and the Italian peninsula, and some realization of the daring and originality displayed by the great Carthaginian general in crossing the Alps with his cumbersome army and attacking Rome from the north. We could not well appreciate the achievements of Columbus if we were ignorant of social and religious conditions in Italy, Portugal and Spain at the time in which he carried on his explorations. We should get a wrong idea of Washington if we neglected to learn how the colonies broke away from England, how the Continental Army was organized and equipped and how France came to the aid of the struggling Revolutionists. We might well make this a principle to guide us in the study of biography: *If we do not know the times, we do not know the man.*

Now a saint, like every other great man, must be studied against the background of the time in which he lives. The saints in every age are much alike, because every saint loves God and his fellowman and is devoted to the Church and labors for the salvation of souls; but the saints in every age are different, too, because social conditions are different, and different times in the world's history have different tendencies and different needs.   Once there was a time in Europe when holy men used to go around collecting money to ransom captives; that is, to buy back men who had been taken away from their homes and made slaves.   If those holy men were living in our country to-day they certainly would not be interested in ransoming captives, for there are no captives to ransom; but they might devote themselves to building hospitals and asylums or conducting clubs for workingmen or giving lectures to non-Catholics.   The interior life of the saint is pretty much the same in every age, for it is a life of holiness and prayer; but the external life of the saint must differ according to the requirements of the age and the country in which he lives.

And so, before we take up the life of St. John Baptist de la Salle and see in what ways he grew in holiness and what things he did for God and the Church, we must glance at the seventeenth century in France, the age and the country in which he labored at the work of God; we must try to find out how the people lived and thought and in what ways they were different from the people of our day. This chapter must be like a moving picture which shows us another country and another time; and, if we use our imaginations as we read, we shall be able to see what France was like, in city and in country, in the days when King Louis XIV held court at Versailles and St. John Baptist de la Salle conducted schools at Reims.

.The first thing that we notice is that the social system was very different from ours. At all times and in every place there are, of course, several classes of people, such as the rich, the fairly rich, and the poor; the learned, the moderately learned, and the ignorant; those who work with their brains, those who work with their hands, and those who do not work at all. Such classes of people were in France in the days of St. de la Salle, just as they are in the United States in our own time. But there was then a class distinction which is not found among us, the distinction between the nobles and the common people, the aristocrats and the artisans or workmen.

What was that distinction? Well, some men were born of noble families—their fathers and grandfathers and great-grandfathers had been called viscounts or marquises or dukes—and so they were for that reason aristocrats; and they were thought, and they thought themselves, better and more important persons just on that account. The aristocrats might study or write or command a regiment in the king's army; but it was considered unworthy and undignified for them to do any manual work or engage in business; and they always wore a certain kind of dress to distinguish them from the common people. And the common people were common people just because their ancestors were butchers or bakers or candlestick makers. Their duty was to honor the aristocrats and work for them and pay their bills; it was considered most improper for them to want to wear the silk stockings of the nobility or to be dissatisfied with their own station in life. When we understand all this we are able to see that St. John Baptist de la Salle, who came of a noble family, did a brave and heroic thing when he devoted his life to the education of the children of the common people.

In two places only the nobles and the commoners met on relatively equal terms—in the church and in the street. The streets of the larger cities such as Paris or Reims or Rouen were winding and narrow, dusty in summer and muddy in winter, paved with irregular cobble-stones and lined by houses which often hung far out into the air. Modern ideas of supplying clean water and of disposing of dirty water were not known, and the visitor who insisted on walking about had need to be on his guard against cascades of soapsuds and showers of refuse from upper windows. The nearest approach to a sewer was an open trench dug along the middle of the street, in which dogs frisked and into which children slipped. Traffic policemen were not a seventeenth century institution, so the streets presented a confusing and exciting spectacle with rearing horses, gilded coaches, squabbling servants, fruit venders shouting their wares and monks in their somber habits picking their way through the throng. At night the streets were dark, and respectable people never ventured forth. A law provided for a candle in every window, but nobody paid any attention to it; and though King Louis did something in Paris to widen, clean and light the streets, in other French cities the night was, in more ways than one, dedicated to the powers of darkness.

But in the daytime, along the streets and in the shops on either side, the city dwellers who were not of the nobility went about their daily tasks. And what did they do? And could any man who wished to, be a tailor or a baker or a locksmith? Not at all. The tradesmen were banded together into guilds which were something like our modern labor unions, one difference being that in the guilds there were only a limited number of members, and applicants had to wait until vacancies occurred. If a young man wished to become a carpenter, for instance, he must first be accepted as an apprentice and work for several years without pay. Then, were a vacancy available, he would become a journeyman, and after several years more, again if there happened to be a vacancy—and usually there was not—he was elevated to the rank of master carpenter. But there were not many master tradesmen; and as they controlled the market, they were not anxious to have their numbers increased. The consequence of it all was that many a man who would have been glad to learn a trade was obliged to remain an unskilled laborer; and as there were thousands of unskilled laborers and very little for them to do, the cities were infested with beggars and pickpockets and sneak thieves, and the roads leading into the country were never free from prowling robbers. We know of two occasions when robbers set upon St. de la Salle, even though they knew him to be a priest.

Of course many poor men, no matter how much they needed food and money, had too much respect for God and His law to do anything wrong, but

earned a few trifling coins by running errands or
holding horses or carrying parcels. The families of
such men were miserable in the extreme. Often
they dwelt huddled together in one small and ill
ventilated room; sometimes they could get no
shelter but the arch of a bridge or the uncovered
roof of a seven-story house. We know for a fact
that a little before the death of Louis XIV, in Rouen,
a city with a population of seven hundred thousand,
some six hundred and fifty thousand people had
only straw bundles for beds.

The common people in the country fared no
better. The farmer did not own the ground he tilled.
The farm was the property of the landed aristocrat
who did no work but took a goodly share of the
products. The king's officers taxed the peasantry
again and again, for money was needed for the
state, and the king and his nobles must be amused
at Versailles. The privilege of collecting the taxes
in country districts was sold at auction to the highest
bidders. The newly made officials paid the money
out of their own pockets, and then, with a license
from the king to collect in the royal name, proceeded
to make themselves rich at the expense of the country
folks. Should the poor people have no money to
give, the king's bailiffs seized the live stock and
imprisoned the peasants. Then the women and
children had to do the farm work; and even country
priests were seen dragging the plow to keep their
parishioners from starving. The peasants rarely
tasted meat; and in famine years many of them
subsisted on a bread made from ferns. To make

matters worse, the king's soldiers sometimes overran the country districts, commandeering whatever was worth the taking.

Meanwhile life was gay and luxurious in the royal palace at Versailles. Ladies in ample gowns of silk and embroidery, and nobles in bright-colored clothes with lace at sleeve and knee, danced and feasted and sang the praises of the Great King. Thither artists came to show their skill, and philosophers to unfold their wisdom. The king was the state, he was the absolute ruler of his land; and so it was his policy to draw the nobles to Versailles, keep them amused, and prevent them from taking undue interest in the affairs of their hereditary estates. His police had the power to arrest any man, common or noble, on mere suspicion, to keep him in confinement as long as they wished, and to prevent him from having any communication with his family and friends. Under such circumstances he was a brave man indeed who defied the will of the sovereign and his favorites.

And yet, that seventeenth century in which King Louis XIV reigned goes down in history as the Golden Age of France. Rarely, if ever, in the history of the world have so many great men lived at the same time. Lending radiance to the name of the Great King were military commanders like Condé, Turenne, and Vendome; architects like Mansard, Blondel and Perrault; painters like Poussin and Le Brun; dramatists like Corneille, Racine and Moliere; poets like Boileau; navigators like Duquesne and Trouville. Immortal names are these,

names that France and the world will never willingly
forget; and even before the Great King's death they
were recognized as immortal. The court of King
Louis XIV was the one glittering point about which
all Europe of the seventeenth century revolved, the
center of refinement and elegance, of wit and wisdom,
of fashion and art.

And—save for some Protestants in the south of
France, the Huguenots—France, both in town and
in country, at court and in the provinces, was a
Catholic land. Every noble family prided itself on
having a son a priest, and every peasant mother
cherished the hope that her boy might some day
dedicate himself to God. The Church received
every outward mark of honor and esteem. Splendid
religious processions, fragrant with incense, bright
with tapers, and melodic with sacred chants, trailed
their glittering length along the crooked streets of
the cities, and from the tiny village churches in the
provinces the priest went solemnly forth to bless the
harvest fields. Few men and women, even in high
places, sought exemption from the fast of Lent,
and to miss Mass was not only a sin but a disgrace.

Nevertheless, both in town and country, many
of the people were ignorant of the truths of salvation.
Some of them went to church and said the public
prayers without any very clear idea of what it all
meant—just as an American boy might enjoy a
holiday on the Fourth of July without much knowledge of the meaning of our national independence.
The nobles in large numbers heard Mass, not on
Sundays only, but every day, and in that they did

well; but many of their after hours were spent in sinful amusements. One lady, for a long time connected with the court of the king, was noted for her alms to the poor, for her visits to religious houses, for her acts of Christian mortification; and all the time she was living in open and shameless sin. The king himself had set the example of ignoring one of God's Commandments; his courtiers were only too willing to follow suit.

But it must not be supposed that all the people, or even most of the people of France, were careless about their duties as Christians. On the contrary, there were many strong and fervent Catholics, many zealous priests, many prayerful monks and nuns, many women of noble birth distinguished for their boundless charity toward the poor. Two of the glories of the reign of Louis XIV are the learned and devoted bishops, Bossuet and Fenelon, the one among the world's supreme orators, the other a writer whose fame will endure as long as the beautiful French language in which he wrote. Then, too, there was one of the most remarkable saints of the Catholic Church, St. Vincent de Paul, who labored so long and so faithfully among the poor in city and country, who founded an order of priests to give missions and an order of Sisters, the well known Daughters of Charity, to teach little children and to care for the sick. The Blessed Louise de Marillac, the co-foundress of the Daughters of Charity, placed her wealth and her talents at the service of the Church and labored for the poor and the unfortunate. The Blessed John Eudes, a saintly priest, devoted his long life to giving missions throughout France, to guiding and encouraging repentant sinners and to organizing and training young priests for parish work.

And there was our own St. John Baptist de la Salle.

CHAPTER III
THE BOYHOOD OF A SAINT

IT has been said that in four different sections of the United States the inhabitants greet the stranger within their gates with four distinctive questions, the questions disclosing what qualities are most esteemed in the several localities. In New England, where learning is given special honor, the question is, "What do you know?" In the Eastern States, the center of the nation's business life, the query takes the form of, "How much have you got?" In the West, which is a relatively pioneer community, they ask, "What can you do?" And in the South, the section where a man's ancestry is felt to be a matter of prime importance, they tactfully inquire, "Who are you?"

In seventeenth century France the attitude was the Southern attitude; then, indeed, the supreme consideration was a man's family tree. If a man had noble ancestors, he was a noble; and to be a noble, to be an aristocrat, was the desirable thing. So it is not surprising to find the early biographers of St. John Baptist de la Salle laying much emphasis on the fact that the founder of the Brothers of the Christian Schools belonged to the illustrious house of de la Salle, which centuries before had come from Spain, and had been recognized among the French aristocracy since the year 1300. It was a family noted for its statesmen, its merchant princes and its fighting men; and its coat-of-arms recalled an old legend according to which an ancestor of the saint, also named John, had had both his legs broken in battle while fighting, in the ninth century, by the side of the Spanish monarch, Alfonso the Chaste. On his mother's side, the saint was descended from the Moëts of Brouillet, another line of aristocrats, many of whom had reflected credit on the legal profession.

Louis de la Salle, the saint's father, was a counsellor-at-law at Reims, and it was in that city that John Baptist was born, April 30, 1651. He was baptized on the very day of his birth in the Church of St. Hilary. He was the oldest child in a family of ten, of whom three died in infancy.

We should like to know more about the early years of little John Baptist, the future samt who was destined to add more glory to the name of de la Salle than had any of his distinguished ancestors; but we are able to secure but a few glimpses of that boyhood which was the seedtime of his future greatness and holiness. The family, belonging as they did to the learned professional class, led a quiet, dignified life, and the boy was taught by his father the importance of walking and speaking and dressing properly and of observing the rules of etiquette at home and in the street, at study and at meals. The elder de la Salle was very fond of music and weekly recitals by the most eminent musicians of Reims were given in his house. He had his son take lessons at an early age; but the boy showed little liking for any harmonies save pious hymns and the official chants of the Church. His mother herself taught him to read; and, what is more important still, encouraged him to learn and say his prayers and to fear mortal sin as the greatest evil in all the world.

An old song has it that "a boy's best friend is his mother"; which is doubtless true. But we must not forget that a boy's very good friend is his grandmother. Little John Baptist's grandmother—his mother's mother—was the comrade of the boy when his father was in the courts and when his mother was busy superintending the servants in the great house; and this grandmother John Baptist loved during all his life. Many years later, when he had grown to be a man and a priest, and was so ill that nobody was allowed to see him, he heard that his grandmother had come to pay him a visit. Though hardly able to stand, he insisted on dressing himself and going down to the parlor in order not to disappoint the dear old friend and companion of his boyhood days.

That his grandmother was truly the friend and companion of John Baptist we know from one interesting little story of his boyhood. One day his father and mother were giving a great feast in honor of friends of the family, and everybody was having a very enjoyable time. The age of King Louis XIV was an age of frequent festivities among the nobility, and all the guests made merry with the banquet and the music and the dancing. But little John Baptist did not like all the noise and confusion and strange faces, so he slipped over to his grandmother and drew her away from the merrymaking throng and asked her to read something for him. Of course she complied with his request—grandmothers always do; and so while the laughter and the music echoed from other parts of the house, the dear old lady and the little boy sat quietly in a retired room, bending over a book that is one of the most interesting books ever written, the Lives of the Saints.

If we would learn to know and to like St. John Baptist de la Salle, we must hang that picture in the gallery of our memory, the picture of the little lad listening to the reading of the Lives of the Saints. Already he had discovered that that book is a wonderful, an absorbing book; he did not find it dull or dry or tiresome, because he liked to hear about the men and women who had done mighty things for God and His Holy Church. Already the little boy had discovered that the saints are true heroes and that their lives are full of thrills and excitement; that when the saints fought against sin and temptation they were doing something more remarkable than soldiers who fight against human foes; that when the saints preached the Gospel or taught little children or cared for the sick they were doing something greater than explorers and scientists and inventors do for mankind.

Often we can tell from the favorite games of a boy what his true vocation in life is, what special talents he has,-and what God wants him to do. When King Louis XIV was a little boy he liked above all things to play soldier, to make his companions march and engage in sham battles; and he never wanted anybody but himself to be the victorious general. His favorite game showed the bent of his mind. He was a bossy sort of boy; and he was a very bossy sort of king; and in 1678, after his victorious campaign in Holland, Louis XIV was acknowledged to have the most numerous, the best drilled, and the best equipped army in Europe.

Little John Baptist de la Salle did not like to play soldier. But he did like to play priest, and often he would drape himself with pieces of cloth to represent the sacred vestments and with great solemnity go through the ceremonies of the Mass. This would have been wrong, of course, if he had intended to make fun of the holy sacrifice; but he was far from doing anything like that. His "playing priest" simply showed that he was more interested in sacred things than in anything else, and that he liked to dream of himself as a minister of God standing before God's holy altar. Every boy has day-dreams of one sort or another—day-dreams in which he pictures himself doing the things he would like best to do; and happy are those boys, in our day and in every day, who have such clean and holy day-dreams as those of St. de la Salle.

Reims was, and is, a wonderful city, its history dating back through many centuries, its streets alive with memories of the past; the city that has the great St. Remigius as its patron; the city whose massive Cathedral of Our Lady was one of the most beautiful pieces of architecture in the world; the city where St. Joan of Arc had her moment of glad triumph when King Charles was crowned. Saints and scholars and statesmen, their fame heralded throughout France and the world, claimed Reims as their home city; and, because it stands so near the frontiers, soldiers time and again passed through its streets to the sound of inspiring music and the cheers of the populace. It was a city where a boy could find many things to see and many things to do, even though in those days little boys, especially the children of noble families, were not allowed as much liberty as American boys of corresponding age.

When John Baptist was nine years of age he began to go to school. He was sent by his parents to what we should call to-day a preparatory school of the University of Reims, the College of Good Children. You will notice that in former years the word *college* was applied to schools which in our tim would be called grammar schools or academies. Here he followed a nine years' course, learning, among other things, grammar, literature, poetry, rhetoric and philosophy. The school was con ducted by priests, so a sound course in religion wa provided and the students were taught to be goo as well as to be studious. Both boarders and day students attended the classes; John Baptist was day-student.

We can picture the boy bidding a morning *a revoir* to his mother and grandmother and startin on his way to school. Since all his biographers tel us he was a thoroughly good boy and a model stu dent, we are safe in assuming that he is not late fo his classes, which began usually at eight and some- times earlier. He is dressed, according to the fashion of the day, in bright colored clothes of fine material—a plum-colored coat fitting close to the waist, the skirts falling over the thighs; light blue knickerbockers, amply cut, and tied at the knee with a rosette of black or maroon; white silk stockings; low-cut, square-toed black shoes with silver buckles, and a heavy three-cornered hat of black felt ornamented in front with a bit of blue and silver ribbon. The school day was a long one, the classes generally continuing until five o'clock. The boy liked his studies and made rapid progress in them; and he never lost the habit of studying. All his life long, St. de la Salle was a student.

But though he liked the College of Good Children, there was one place in the great city of Reims that little John Baptist liked even more. That was the Church of St. Hilary, whither his mother or his grandmother used to take him to vespers and to Mass. He loved to listen to the solemn chants of the Church, he was fascinated by the lights and the ceremonies, the odor of incense was sweet in his nostrils. And then one day he received permission to enroll himself among the altar boys and serve the priest at Mass. He was a very happy lad when for the first time he buttoned up his little black cassock, donned his white surplice, and took his place with the other servers. In the performance of his duties as altar boy he was most punctual and attentive. "He attracted," we are told, "the attention of all the assistants and inspired all the beholders with devotion."

This fleeting picture of St. John Baptist de la

Salle as a boy may be disappointing to some of us who expect to find the boyhood of a saint different from the boyhood of other men. But if we have such expectations, we are wrong. As boys and as men the saints did not generally do such wonderful and unusual things; or, if they did, they are not saints on that account. No, they did the common, the usual, the ordinary things; but—and here is the secret of their sainthood—they did everything as well as they knew how. Not what we do, but how we do it—that is what makes us saints!

CHAPTER IV
TO THE ALTAR OF GOD

WE are told in the Bible that the Prophet Samuel, when a little boy, heard the voice of God calling him by name. At first he thought the summons came from his master, the high priest, Heli; but when he was assured that the call was coming to him direct from Heaven, the lad promptly and whole-heartedly answered, "Speak, Lord, for Thy servant heareth!" And then God told him what He wanted him to do.

The call that came to Samuel is what is known as vocation—God asking the soul to do something for His honor and glory. It is a request, and not a command; but those who really and truly love God are glad and happy to comply in all things with God's holy will. The saints have been saints largely because they have been attentive to the voice of God and eager to do anything and everything that God asks them to do.

It is a fact which little John Baptist de la Salle must have learned when he listened to his grandmother read the Lives of the Saints, that very many holy men received the call from God while they were still in their early youth. The Lives of the Saints contain many instances of vocation coming at an early age; and the Holy Scriptures tell us that those are blessed who have borne the yoke of the Lord

from their youth. A boyhood spent in obedience to
parents and devotion to duty is the best preparation
for a call from God. For that call is like the seed
which Our Lord spoke about in the Gospel. No
matter how good the seed is in itself, it will not take
root and grow and bear fruit if it falls in the road-
way or on the rocks or among the thorns. It will
be dried up or eaten by the birds of the air unless
it falls on good ground.

The soul of young de la Salle—that soul never
stained by mortal sin—was good ground; and so,
when the call came to him he was prompt to answer.
Like the little Samuel he was ready to say, "Speak,
Lord, for Thy servant heareth!" His liking for the
Lives of the Saints, his faithfulness to his studies,
his habits of prompt and cheerful obedience, his
interest in the ceremonies of the Church—all these
things gave evidence of his fitness for a life dedicated
to the service of God; and when he heard in his
heart a still, small voice asking him to take upon his
young shoulders the yoke of the Lord, he did not
put off his decision. One day, when he was only
eleven years old, he went to his father and said,

"My father, I wish to be a priest."

His father, who was both wise and good, knew
that it is very dangerous for parents to interfere, one
way or the other, in the vocation of their children.
He knew, as the poet Browning says,

> " 'Tis an awkward thing to play with souls,
> And matter enough to save one's own."

He knew that his boy was rather young to make a

decision which would affect the whole course of his life; but, on the other hand, he knew that God often speaks to little ones and calls them in the flush of their youth to His holy service. In any case, he knew that many years must pass before John Baptist could be ordained sub-deacon, and that at any time previous to that event the boy might alter his decision if he wished. We may even suppose that the father would not be very much disappointed if the lad did change his mind, that, while he would be glad to see his son a zealous priest, he would not be sorry were the boy to remain in the world.

For—and here is another thing about the seventeenth century that we must not overlook—parents generally did not want their eldest son to become a priest or a religious. Every noble family was glad to have representatives among the clergy and in the great religious orders, but there were generally plenty of younger sons to answer the call of the Lord. It was a custom of the time for the eldest son to assist the father in the direction of the family, to take upon his shoulders the same professional cares and to uphold the honor of the family name. As a matter of fact, as we shall soon see, John Baptist's ordination was delayed on account of his family responsibilities. God was very good to the family of the de la Salles, for two of the saint's brothers became priests and one of his sisters became a nun.

In the city of St. de la Salle's birth was a body of men known as canons. The canons, all either priests or candidates for the priesthood, wore a special costume, recited the Divine Office in the cathedral, and led a life of stricter regularity than ordinary secular priests. It was considered a great honor to be chosen a canon.

When he was only fifteen years of age, that honor came to St. de la Salle. Canon Dozet, a relative of the de la Salles, had grown old, and the idea came to him of resigning his canonry in favor of some rightly disposed young man. He had known John Baptist from babyhood, had observed his youthful piety and purity of life, had applauded his wish to become a priest. He had noted, too, that the youth's name was listed among the honor students of the college. All this moved him to resign his seat among the canons in favor of de la Salle, and the young man was solemnly installed a Canon of Reims early in 1667.

The saint now realized that his work of preparation for the holy priesthood must take two forms: He must become a learned man, and he must become a holy man. He continued his studies at the University of Reims and received the degree of master of arts in 1669. He then entered on his course in theology at the university of his native city; but his father decided that for so brilliant and attentive a student the best was none too good, so he sent him to the celebrated school known as the Sorbonne, in Paris, where he had the privilege of studying under the ablest and most renowned teachers in France. He passed his final examinations in Reims and secured the degree of doctor in 1680. That degree was then, as it is to-day, the highest evidence of scholarship and research, and it secured for the founder of the Christian Brothers a place in the ranks of the learned.

But St. de la Salle well knew that learning, though necessary for the priest, is not the only need. The priest is the ambassador of Christ, another Christ, whose responsibility it is to be an example in all things to the members of the flock of the Lord. He must be holy as well as learned, deep in prayer as well as in books, knowing the path of goodness not less than the path of lore. So he attended likewise another famous school in Paris, the seminary of St. Sulpice.

The Sulpician Fathers are a body of priests, founded in the seventeenth century by Father Olier, who do a very special work in the Church. Every order makes some one thing the special end of its efforts. Thus, the Dominicans devote themselves especially to preaching, the Trappists to prayer and penance, the Paulists to giving missions to Catholics and to non-Catholics. But the Sulpicians do something different still. They give their time and their energy and their learning to the training of priests, to the proper education of young men who feel called to the ecclesiastical state. Some of the most saintly and highly educated men the world has known in the last two hundred years were Sulpicians.

The seminary of St. Sulpice was a school of sanctity; and there, in company with several young men who afterward became famous, notably Fenelon, the holy Archbishop of Cambrai, St. John Baptist de la Salle learned the science of the saints. Years afterward, the superior of the seminary wrote of him as follows:

"His conversation was always gentle and becoming. He appeared to me never to have displeased any one, or to have drawn on himself any censure. When he came to Paris for his studies, I noticed that he had made marvelous progress in all the virtues."

A great sorrow came to John Baptist in 1671, when his mother died at Reims. Holiness does not —or, at least, should not—freeze up the affection the saints have for their dear ones, and St. de la Salle loved tenderly the noble lady who had taught him so much and had helped to form his character. Though history tells us but little of Madame de la Salle, we know enough about her to realize that she was a fine type of the Christian mother, a queen in her household, the companion of her children, and an example to all in piety and devotion to duty. No great man—be he saint or artist or statesman— ever became great without the assistance of some woman; and in the case of St. de la Salle the woman was his loving and devoted mother.

A year later the saint's father died. It would seem as though God, to try the young man's character and test his virtue, was giving him sorrow upon sorrow. Such has often been God's way with His chosen ones, that out of their trouble good may come and that after their sadness they may rejoice forever. Sorrow, as the Catholic poet, Francis Thompson, has finely said, is "but shade of His Hand, outstretched caressingly.

The death of his father caused St. de la Salle to interrupt his studies, for he was the eldest son and it was necessary for him to take charge of his brothers and sisters, some of whom were still mere children. So he left his beloved St. Sulpice and returned to Reims and for six years acted as the administrator of the family. And here is another thing worthy of our attention; his holiness did not prevent his having an excellent head for business. He was prudent and capable in money matters as well as in family affairs. In this respect he reminds us of St. Teresa, who was at once the most eminent saint of her time, the greatest woman writer in the world, and the most efficient business manager in Spain.

Doubts concerning his vocation to the priesthood came to him about this time, and for a while he wondered whether or not he was doing the right thing in persevering in his youthful intention of dedicating himself to God. It was most natural that the cares and worries incident to his business responsibilities should have had this effect on him. But he thought the matter out thoroughly, looking at it from every side; he prayed that he might learn and do the holy will of God, and he took the advice of competent friends and guides. The result was that his scruples disappeared and he saw, more clearly than ever before, that the call he had heard while still a little boy had really come from God. He now bent every energy and every talent in one direction: He was determined to be a priest and a very good one.

Slowly and carefully he prepared himself for ordination. He felt, as he approached unto the altar of God, the truth of the holy words: "How terrible is this place! This is no other than the house of God and the gate of heaven." He remembered that some of the holiest men who ever lived trembled at the thought of the awful responsibilities and the sublime dignity of the Catholic priest; that the singing saint of Italy, Francis of Assisi, through humility refused to take the final step; and that St. Vincent de Paul had exclaimed: "Had I known what a priest is, I should never have consented to become one."

The happiest day in his long and troubled life was Holy Saturday, April 9, 1678, the sixth anniversary of his father's death. On that day he was ordained a priest in the historic Cathedral of Reims and for the first time exercised the priest's most august function of changing the bread and wine into the Body and Blood of Our Blessed Lord. And his first Mass he offered in one of the cathedral chapels with intense devotion and fervor.

From that blissful day the holy sacrifice of the Mass became and remained his one supreme consolation. In the future years he never failed to celebrate daily, no matter how ill or weary he might be, or how far away from home.

He had approached unto the altar of God; and God had given joy to his youth.

CHAPTER V
THE MAN FROM ROUEN

WHEN the Most Blessed Virgin Mary was a little girl the time for the coming of the Redeemer, as indicated in the prophecies of the Old Testament, had almost arrived, and many a mother among the Hebrew people, and many a young girl who looked forward to motherhood as the glory of her earthly life, hoped against hope to become the mother of the Expected of the Nations. Because she was so pure of soul and bright of mind, Mary thought little of herself, and did not even dream that the great honor would come to her. But we may be sure that she prayed, and prayed earnestly, that the Messias might come, and that the world might be redeemed. Little did she think, as thus she prayed, that her prayers were hastening the season of her own seven sorrows and her own surpassing glory as Mother of God.

When St. John Baptist de la Salle was studying for the priesthood under the Sulpician Fathers he had joined a little society, composed of seminarians, the object of which was to pray that more Christian teachers might be given to the children of France. This society had been organized by a devout priest whose experience in the confessional and elsewhere had shown him that many sins might be prevented and many troubles removed and many lives made

pleasing to God, if only the teachers of boys and girls
were wiser and better. And so he induced the young
men at St. Sulpice to form themselves into an army
of prayer to ask God to bless the land with good
teachers and good schools.

St. de la Salle little dreamed, when he prayed for
the blessing of Christian education, that he himself
would be the answer to the prayers, that already
God had chosen him to be the founder of a society
of teachers who would conduct Christian schools in
France and throughout the world, that in the years
to come he himself would be hailed as the patron
saint of popular education and as an authority on the
organization of schools and the training of teachers.

For, although at a very early age John Baptist
felt that God wanted him to be a priest, he had
no idea whatever that God likewise wanted him to
be an educator. All young men, even saints, sometimes like to fancy themselves older and wiser and
better, like to think of themselves as doing something worth while in the world; and, doubtless,
John Baptist had his little day-dreams, too. Perhaps he pictured himself as a priest laboring in the
confessional reconciling sinners to God, or in the
pulpit preaching impressive sermons, or in the
streets of his native city visiting the poor and the
sick; but certainly he never pictured himself teaching in a schoolroom. Yet it was to the schoolroom
that God called him.

At the time, after his father's death, that the
saint was in Reims taking care of his younger
brothers and preparing himself for ordination, he

had a friend and father confessor, named Nicholas Roland. This Father Roland was a saintly man who prayed and labored much in the interests of God. A work in which he was especially interested was the education of little girls. He had taken charge of some orphan girls and devoted much of his attention to teaching them the truths of holy religion and imparting to them instruction in such secular subjects as would be of value to them in after life. This work grew so fast that Father Roland could not carry it on himself, so he interested several ladies in the schools which he had founded. The number of his assistants increased, and after a while they banded themselves into a society which was directed by the zealous priest. They were really a community of teaching Sisters, and were known as the Sisters of the Holy Child Jesus.

Father Roland was just in the prime of life, at the age of thirty-five, when he grew very sick, and only a few days after St. de la Salle had been ordained priest, the founder of the Sisters went to his heavenly reward. One of the last things he did before his death was to ask his young and fervent friend, Canon de la Salle, to take care of the Sisters and their schools. How could the young priest refuse this last request of a dying man? He promised his friend that he would look after the interests of the Community of the Holy Child Jesus and that he would superintend the educational work in which the nuns were engaged.

And he was faithful to his promise. The ladies who taught in the schools founded by Father Roland were not yet officially recognized as religious teachers, and so St. de la Salle undertook the difficult work of having them accepted as a teaching community by both Church and State. He used his tact and his knowledge of human nature, he appealed for assistance to influential family friends, he pleaded the cause of the Sisters before the city council; and presently he received the approbation of the Archbishop of Paris and a license or permission, known as letters patent, from King Louis XIV.

In that way the work of the Community of the Holy Child Jesus was solidly established, Father Roland's life ambition was realized, and opportunities for education were secured for the little girls of the city of Reims.

Then, though St. John Baptist de la Salle continued to interest himself in the schools started by Father Roland, the work of the teachers was now running smoothly, and he found time to devote himself almost entirely to his priestly duties and to his studies, for at this time he was still preparing to receive the doctor's cap. It never occurred to him that the promise he had made to his dying friend was the first step toward fulfilling the will of God in his own regard, that from now on he was destined to be an educator and a trainer of teachers, and that his life was to be devoted to the education of boys. Many years afterward the saint said, "Had I known what was in store for me, I think I should have given up the work." It is as true of saints, as of anybody else that, as Bulwer-Lytton has said, "The veil which covers the face of futurity was woven by the hand of mercy."

One day when St. de la Salle went to pay a visit to Father Roland's nuns, he met there a man, fifty-nine years old, travel-stained and weary, accompanied by a lad of fourteen. The man's name was Adrian Nyel, and he had come to Reims to open a school for boys. He was to be principal and first class teacher, and the lad he brought with him was to be his assistant. Nyel had heard of the fine work done by the Sisters of the Holy Child Jesus, and of the capable direction which Canon de la Salle had given the schools; and so he wanted advice and assistance before starting his own educational work.

But why had Nyel come to Reims? The answer to this question brings us to an interesting story. There lived in the city of Rouen a wealthy lady, a distant relative of St. de le Salle, whose name was Madame de Maillefer. She had led a life of idleness and vanity, and, like many great ladies of her time, expended vast sums of money on her clothes and her carriages, her gardens and her banquets. Though poor people were starving all around her, she gave them but little attention and sought only her own selfish pleasure.

One day a beggar came to her and asked her for help. She told the poor man to go about his business; but he was so ill and weak that he could hardly stagger from the rich lady's door. Madame de Maillefer's coachman took the beggar into a stable to rest, and there he died. The mistress was very angry when she heard of the kind act of her servant, and after giving him a severe scolding, dismissed him from her service. As the coachman slowly left the room the lady threw an old cloak after him, telling him to bury the beggar in that.

The beggar was duly buried; and that evening Madame de Maillefer was about to seat herself at table when she discovered something lying directly in front of her. It was the cloak which she had thrown after the coachman. Again she was very angry and she asked her servants for an explanation. They all professed to know nothing about the cloak, except that several of them were sure that it had been wrapped about the beggar's body before burial. To them and to her it looked as though the dead beggar had spurned the alms which the rich lady had so grudgingly given him; that since she had refused him a bit of bread in life, he declined to accept her cloak in death.

Madame de Maillefer began to think about this, and day by day she came to see that she had been unkind to the poor man, and to many other poor people; that she had been mean and selfish and sinful. Gradually her entire life changed. She who had been so worldly and vain became religious and humble. She wore simple clothing, sold her expensive furniture and carriages, and devoted herself to the care of the poor and the sick. The remainder of her life was given to works of Christian charity, including the education of needy children.

Madame de Maillefer gave much of her money to establish schools in Rouen; and after a time she desired to assist the poor children in other cities as well. She knew of the educational work conducted by Adrian Nyel, and so she promised to furnish financial support to his school provided he would open one for the boys of Reims. That explains why Nyel came to Reims and why he carried a letter of introduction from Madame de Maillefer to her relative, Canon de la Salle.

The unlooked for meeting of the saint and Adrian Nyel in the reception room of the Sisters of the Holy Child Jesus was the beginning of a long and fruitful comradeship between the two men, so different in training and disposition. In many respects one was the opposite of the other. Canon de la Salle was of the aristocracy; Nyel was of the people. One was a priest, the other a layman. One was highly educated, the other but very moderately so. St. de la Salle was of a cast of mind cautious, prudent, deliberate; Nyel was sanguine, impulsive, even headstrong; the canon was characterized by delicacy and refinement of manners; the teacher was brusque and common. St. de la Salle was not thirty years old; Adrian Nyel was almost sixty.

Despite these differences of education, character, and outlook on life, God brought the two men together to serve His holy purpose, and from the first they liked each other immensely. Nyel, now that he had met and spoken with Canon de la Salle, felt that there would be no especial difficulties in establishing a school in Reims; and the saint was so captivated by the optimism and enthusiasm of the visitor that he insisted on taking him into his house as a guest.

"Come to me," said the saint to Nyel. "Visiting priests are in the habit of staying at my home;

and," he added, with a delicate touch of humor impossible to resist, "you look just like a country pastor."

And so the man from Rouen and his boy assistant found themselves guests in the stately and aristocratic mansion of the de la Salles. The teacher had entered the home of the Canon of Reims.

CHAPTER VI
THE FIRST TEACHERS

ADRIAN NYEL was the sort of man that people to-day would call a hustler. He liked to get results and get them right away, and while doing one thing he had his eye fixed on the next thing to do. He soon had several schools for boys established in Reims, and his one little assistant had been succeeded by a dozen or more teachers. Charitable people of the city began to interest themselves in educational work, and more than one wealthy lady gave money for the foundation of new schools. Nyel was delighted, and looked forward to a time when his schools would be established in other cities of France. Though an old man, this energetic founder of schools had a young man's fondness for dreaming dreams.

St. de la Salle was more cautious. He must have been amused very often by his comrade's whirlwind activity and unquenchable cheerfulness, but he saw clearly that the work which so absorbed the time and attention of Adrian Nyel would burst like a bubble unless it were more rigidly organized and more carefully supervised. Though he recognized as completely as anybody the crying need for the schools, he did not like the rapidity with which they were being opened; for he recognized something else—something which Nyel had failed to take into account. That something was the necessity of training the teachers.

We shall never understand what St. de la Salle did in the field of education, the greatness of his sacrifices, or the high quality of his work, we shall never grasp the true significance of educational problems in the seventeenth century, unless we know the sort of men who did the bulk of elementary teaching in the days of Louis XIV. The Jesuits and other capable men conducted colleges and universities, but those institutions were intended for the children of the nobility. Who did the teaching for the children of the people?

Some devoted parish priests and their assistants were engaged in the schoolroom, but not many; for teaching is a task that requires practically all of a man's time, and the priest has other duties to perform. Candidates for the priesthood and university students, tiding themselves over a period of financial stringency, would keep school for a while, but they were unsatisfactory because they had no experience and no genuine love for their work. The schools were so poor and the pay given teachers was so low that a man usually would not take up teaching until he had found that he was unfitted for doing anything else. There are exceptions to every rule, but it may justly be said that, prior to the changes wrought by St. John Baptist de la Salle, the teachers in the elementary schools of France represented the survival of the unfittest.

Indeed, anybody, provided he was recognized as knowing a little more than his pupils, was deemed worthy of being called schoolmaster. At Lyons the school was kept by a man who previously had kept a wine shop; elsewhere the ranks of teachers were made up even of jailbirds and undesirable citizens. A pious priest of the day complained that "the greatest number of schoolmistresses are ignorant; among the schoolmasters there are heretics, impious men who have followed impious callings, and under whose guidance the young are in evident danger of being lost." In the face of this testimony we may agree that by no means the worst type of schoolmaster was the jolly-faced fiddler who on occasions would desert his pupils and their studies to go and discourse sweet music at a village wedding.

The teachers gathered—Heaven knows where!—by Adrian Nyel in his efforts to open more and more classes in Reims and other places, were evidently not of the lowest class of pedagogues of the time; but, all the same, most of them were poor specimens. They were ignorant and uncouth, incapable of teaching anything in a really vital way, and unable to form in their pupils enlightened tastes and refined manners. Nyel accepted their services because they were the best teachers he could get; St. de la Salle felt that it was little short of criminal to open more schools until the teachers were themselves taught how to teach and how to live.

The teachers often got on the nerves of the delicately brought up canon; but he pitied their helplessness and did what he could to guide them in their work. And, with that attention to practical needs which many of the saints have evinced, he first of all thought about their stomachs. Though Nyel was doubtless doing his best, they were being poorly and inadequately fed. St. de la Salle, knowing that a teacher cannot afford to have an ill-nourished body, volunteered to supply the masters with food from his own house. The offer was gladly accepted, and thereafter twice a day a string of servants carried trays of food from the de la Salle kitchen to the humble abode of the schoolmasters.

But the saint thought of more than the bodily comfort of the teachers. On every possible occasion he would visit their schools, observe how they taught, give them specimen lessons, and offer helpful advice; and out of school hours he would often call them together and give them practical talks on teaching and on living. His great idea was to make them cultured men, in order that they might become capable teachers. He believed that the important thing about any teacher is not what subjects he teaches or in what grade nor how long he has been engaged in school work, but simply, what sort of man he is. And so he tried to make the teachers of Reims into learned and saintly and manly men.

It was very hard work. Many of Adrian Nyel's recruits had had generation after generation of rude peasantry in their ancestry and they looked upon refined manners as something silly and womanish. They had no taste for study and no great liking for the acts of Christian devotion which the canon recommended them to perform. They knew so little, in short, that they needed somebody to be over them all the time to tell them what to do and how to do it. The educated man is able to make his own decisions and handle the details of his job; the ignorant man can do nothing without assistance, advice, and incessant supervision.

Now, with all their good intentions and excellent dispositions, the schoolmasters were ignorant men, and for a great part of the day, as St. de la Salle regretfully observed, they were left very much to themselves. Nyel was away, somewhere or other, for long periods of time, and when he was at home with the masters his presence was often worse than his absence. For Nyel, though pious and fervent, was an old man, a tired old man; and he and the masters, nearly all very young men, naturally saw things differently. The result was misunderstanding and friction.

All this St. de la Salle realized, and he perceived that unless something were done to educate the teachers more thoroughly and to direct them more tactfully and more regularly, the work of the schools would go to ruin. "If," he thought, "they could take their meals in my house with me, I could have them learn many things quickly and hold them happily together."

The masters take their meals in his house! Yes, it was a noble project; but what an unbending of his aristocratic dignity! To one of his refined manners the prospect of seeing a dozen uncouth young men violating the rules of table etiquette and giving other evidences of lack of breeding was really a cause of suffering. But the good in the idea outweighed the inconvenience and annoyance, and so he extended the invitation, which was promptly accepted. While the teachers were with him he utilized every moment to form them in politeness and piety, and to give them a relish for the things of the mind; and a few weeks saw his labors blessed with excellent results.

Then one day—it was in Holy Week, 1681—Nyel went on a journey somewhat longer than usual, and St. de la Salle found it necessary to take charge of the group of teachers during the absence of the energetic head of the house. The good effects of his week's visit with them were so marked that the young men were frankly delighted, and even Nyel had to compliment them when he managed to rush back from Guise. This impressed St. de la Salle very much, and the thought came to him: "If I am able to do so much with the masters in one week, what might I not accomplish if I brought them into my own house and had them living with me always?"

This thought occupied his mind for a long, long time. He saw that it was the best thing that could happen to the teachers; but what about himself? Would he be justified in extending hospitality to those ill-mannered and unlearned peasants? Their coarse ways repulsed him at table; what would be the state of affairs if he had to tolerate their company not only at meals but throughout the live-long day? His hesitancy can be appreciated only by those who know what a gulf there was between the classes and the masses in seventeenth century France.

St. de la Salle would have liked to turn in his perplexity to his deceased friend, Father Roland; that being impossible, he went to Paris to see another holy priest. This man was Father Barré. After St. de la Salle had told how he had been led, almost against his will and certainly against his inclinations, into the work of the schools, after he had described the plans he was following for the training of the masters and the project of taking them to live with him—a project which made him tremble with disgust and yet which persisted in staying before his mind— Father Barré told him that the school work was manifestly God's work, and that it was surely God's will that Canon de la Salle should carry it to its destined success. "Therefore," he said, "do what your heart prompts you to do—what God tells you to do. Take the masters into your house. You will be criticised for it, and your motives will be misunderstood. But remember that the grandest designs of God are achieved only through contradictions."

And so, on the feast of his holy patron, St. John the Baptist, June 24, 1681, St. de la Salle took the lowly teachers under his ancestral roof.

CHAPTER VII
GRAY DAYS AND GOLD

ST. DE LA SALLE did a brave and heroic thing when he yielded to what was clearly the will of God and took the schoolmasters to live with him in his own house. And God, who dearly loves generous souls, promptly rewarded him for it. Having the teachers close to him day after day, the saint was able to advise and encourage them in their work, to teach them the things it was so necessary that they should know, and to form them to habits of scholarship and devotion. As the farmer, after the toil of ploughing the land and sowing the seed, enjoys the vision of the first tender shoots of grain peeping out of the earth, so St. de la Salle, after suffering inconvenience and annoyance by reason of the presence of the rude young teachers, now rejoiced to see them becoming more like gentlemen in manners and more successful and interested in the work of the schools.

But his troubles were not yet over; really, they had only begun. For long his aristocratic relatives and friends had been shaking their heads over the amount of time he had devoted to Adrian Nyel and his school-teachers. Now and again protests were openly made to the saint. It was all very well, he was told, to have some interest in the education of poor boys and to be kind to the men who did the teaching; but there was a limit to everything. If any priest was to spend most of his time with the schools and the teachers, it should be some simple parish priest who himself had sprung from the people; not the scion of a noble family, a canon of the cathedral and a doctor of the university. And when he went so far as to have the masters take their meals at his table he was told, rather pointedly, that he was carrying his charity altogether too far, and that he should have more regard for the feelings of his younger brothers than to permit the upstart teachers to fraternize with his own kith and kin. If class distinctions were to be ignored, if men like Canon de la Salle did not draw a line somewhere between the nobles and the commoners, what on earth was the world coming to?

But a real storm broke out when the news began to spread—and such news always spreads fast—that Canon de la Salle had actually asked the school-teachers to come, bag and baggage, to live in his ancestral home. A committee of his relatives bore down upon him with a great smoke of indignation and a strong volley of remonstrances. What was he thinking about? Had he lost his senses? Had he no feeling for his dear, dead mother, no respect for the memory of his noble father? Had he no sense of his own dignity as priest and canon and doctor? It was wrong; it was shameful! What did he mean by giving his time and his money and his companion-ship to this gang of boorish fellows who had neither birth nor breeding, and who, for aught he knew, might steal the furniture and the family jewels and decamp over night?

To the members of his family who thus sought to have him turn the teachers out of his house, St. de la Salle did not offer any explanations. He knew they could not, or would not, understand. He knew that his relatives were so blinded by pride of birth and so befogged by class prejudice as to be incapable of appreciating his motives. But he received them courteously, gentleman that he was, and listened to them kindly and patiently, sitting quite at his ease and with his arms folded across his breast. And when they had said their say and flounced out of the door, he went calmly back to his work of teaching the masters.

The schools in Reims were now in a flourishing condition and crowds of boys were being taught, and taught well, by Adrian Nyel's recruits. As for Nyel himself, about this time he disappears forever from the story of St. de la Salle's life and works. Delighted with the progress in learning and sanctity made by the teachers, overjoyed at the sight of the hordes of children flocking to the schools, Nyel, who was first, last and all the time an educational pioneer, left the work entirely in the hands of the saint, and betook himself to pastures new. Not long afterward he died at Rouen, happily—and, we are almost tempted to say, energetically—to the last intent on opening new schools. He had been the human instrument chosen by Almighty God to force the problems of education into the reluctant hands of Canon de la Salle; and now that the saint was identified with those problems and so successfully solving them, Nyel was no longer needed. A good man and true was Adrian Nyel, and his memory will always be cherished by the children of de la Salle.

A school well taught is always its own best advertisement. So it was not long before the success of Canon de la Salle's masters, as they now came to be called, spread beyond the confines of Reims, and other cities sought to have schools conducted by these unusually well-trained teachers. The saint believed in making haste slowly; he determined not to open schools until he had his teachers sufficiently well prepared to teach properly. The work of preparation went on steadily, and after a few months he was able to begin foundations in several cities.

One of his letters, promising to send teachers to Chateau-Porcien, has been preserved; in it he discloses the grace of the gentleman, the practical outlook of the educator, and the piety of the saint:

"Even were I to take but little interest in the glory of God, I should be very hard-hearted not to be touched by the earnest entreaties of your dean and by the courteous manner in which you have addressed me. I should be very wrong, gentlemen, not to send you teachers from our community, seeing your eagerness and ardor to provide Christian instruction and education for your children. Rest assured, then, that I have nothing more at heart than to second your good intentions in this matter and that, next Saturday, I shall send you two teachers to begin the school on the day following the feast of St. Peter. I hope you will be pleased with them."

But a new trial speedily came to the saint, this time from the teachers themselves. It is a sad truth of human nature that under kind treatment some men become restless and insolent. Such was the case with most of the young teachers now enjoying the hospitality of Canon de la Salle.

He had taken them almost literally out of the streets, had sheltered them beneath his own roof, had given them better food than they had ever tasted before in their miserable lives. He had lavished on them, despite his repugnance at their coarseness, his care, his instruction, his advice, and his friendship. He had made them better men and better teachers and more useful members of society. Through his efforts they had attained more respect in the eyes of the public than elementary teachers had ever won. They should have been very happy, very earnest and very grateful.

But, as the wise old proverb has it, "You cannot make a silk purse out of a sow's ear." Almost without exception the masters were crude and common; and though at first the saint's kindness won from them a measure of regard, they presently revealed the lowness of their origin and the uncouthness of their manners by ignoring the unceasing solicitude of their director, by imposing upon his gentleness and courtesy, and by planning to turn the educational and cultural opportunities he was giving them to their own selfish advantage. In brief, now that they were better able to conduct schools than other men engaged in that work, they thought of the money they might be able to demand, and the relatively easeful life they might enjoy; and so all but two of them left the community and went forth to seek their fortunes. Thus the fatherly care bestowed upon them by the saint they repaid with ingratitude and desertion.

Let us, however, not misunderstand their position; let us try to be just to them, at least. They had no religious vows and they were free to go if they wished; but among refined and intelligent and well-bred men there are certain higher obligations, not nominated in the bond, not matters of law or vow, which in honor and decency demand respect. "All things are lawful to me," says St. Paul, "but all things are not expedient." Those first masters of St. de la Salle were too ignorant and too rude to appreciate what the saint had done for them, and too thick-skinned to feel the unexpressed obligations of a gentleman.

Our Blessed Lord Himself suffered keenly from ingratitude; so St. de la Salle, who day by day was learning more and more to follow in the footsteps of His Master, bore this biting sorrow in silence. His teaching staff was perilously diminished, and the training-school for teachers had reached almost the vanishing point; but he did not despair. He knew that if this were not God's work it deserved to perish, and that if it was indeed God's work God would not let it pass away.

And his faith was justified. For as the deserters, in ones and twos, shambled from his door, other young men came, almost miraculously, to take their places. And this second crop of Christian teachers was of a finer vintage. Many of them had a fairly good education; others were of better families.

Several of them, originally intending to study for th
priesthood or the law, decided to join in the work o
the noble canon, for the eyes of youth always shin
at sight of the heroic, and St. de la Salle, in devotin
himself to the cause of the Christian schools, was
doing an eminently heroic thing. So the saint'
house was once more filled with prospective teachers
the gaps in the little army of education were filled
and day by day the recruits, under the direction of
wise and sympathetic commander, were learning th
use of the weapons wielded by scholars and by saints.

CHAPTER VIII
A CHEERFUL GIVER

MANY years before, when St. John Baptist de la Salle was a little boy and listened to his dear grandmother read the Lives of the Saints, he discovered that the holy men and women whom his boyish mind so much admired were noted for two important qualities. How much they might differ in age and occupation, in country and education, in intelligence and general ability, they were all alike distinguished for the spirit of prayer and the spirit of generosity. The saints were experts or specialists when it came to talking with God; and they were open-handed when it came to giving up things for the sake of God. And so God listened to their prayers and blessed their generosity; and so they became saints.

All his life long St. John Baptist de la Salle loved to pray, for in prayer, in conversation with God, he found strength and refreshment and the sweetest delight. But he understood what generosity meant, too; and in this chapter we shall see how he drew down the blessing of God on the work of the Christian Schools by gladly giving up everything that he could possibly give. This chapter is a chapter of sacrifice.

It is true everywhere in the world that everything has its price; that if a man wants to own a house or an automobile or to enjoy a trip to the mountains or the seashore, he has to pay for it. For such things he pays in money. But for the things of the mind he pays in time and energy; a man can become a great historical scholar, for instance, only by studying earnestly hour after hour, day after day. The same law holds good in the life of the soul. If a man wants to gain virtue and merit, if he wants to grow more and more like to God and do great things for God, if, in short, he wants to become a saint, he likewise has to pay for it. And he pays, not in money, nor even in study; he pays by sacrifice. Sacrifice is the com of the Kingdom of Heaven.

St. Peter, the chief of the Apostles, once said to Our Blessed Lord: "Behold, we have left all things and have followed Thee." As a matter of fact, St. Peter had not really given up so very much. He was a poor man and about all he had to leave behind him was a weather-beaten boat with a few old fishing nets. But Our Lord blessed his sacrifice and promised him a measureless reward, because, though he hadn't given up much, yet he had cheerfully given all he had. St. Peter understood the spirit of sacrifice not less than the spirit of prayer.

Just one year to the day after the school-teachers had moved into the de la Salle mansion, they moved out again; and this time the saint went with them. He had found that the mansion, though a fine place for a family to live in, was not suited to the work of teaching the masters to pray and to study and to teach. There were too many distractions, too many annoyances; and after a while there was lack of room. So he secured a plain, large house in New

Street and there set up his little community of instructors. And he left his own house, the home of his ancestors, never more to return.

That was one step toward his supreme sacrifice. Only a man very generous with Almighty God could have done what St. John Baptist de la Salle did on that St. John's day of 1682. Let us consider what it meant. It meant that he, the priest of gentle birth and high education and brilliant prospects, attached himself to the society of men far beneath him in family, in breeding, and in accomplishments. It meant that he cut himself off from the delights of familiar intercourse with his own brothers and sisters and from the numerous family reunions which many of his relatives were accustomed to enjoy in his house. It meant that he renounced all the sweet and tender memories which the house itself contained, the souvenirs of his boyhood days, the antique furniture and decorations, the gleaming silver and sparkling crystal, the portraits and paintings beyond price.

We Americans are prone to underestimate the greatness of this sacrifice so cheerfully made by St. de la Salle, for home meant more to a man in France in the seventeenth century than we can readily understand. It may be said that in one sense we in this country have no homes at all. At least we are always changing our homes. We move from city to city, from state to state; and many a man does not know, and does not especially care, what has become of the house in which he was born. Many of our people live in a succession of rented apartments;

the popular song-writer stated a truth when he
defined home, in the American sense of the word, as
any place where a man hangs his hat.   It is vastly
different in France.   Generally the one house remains
the center of the family life for generation after generation, and it becomes a sacred place, dearer to its
owners than anything else in the wide world.   The
feeling for home, so strong even now in France, was
stronger in the seventeenth century;   and it must
have been especially strong in the heart of a man so
tender and sympathetic as the founder of the Christian Brothers.   For him to give up his home forever
was a sacrifice indeed.

But more still did God demand of him, and more
did he generously give.   Now that he had devoted
himself so wholeheartedly to the labors of the
schools, of what use to him was the title of Canon of
Reims?   To be a canon was a great honor, a great
dignity;   but the office interfered with his plans for
the formation of his teachers, and made heavy
inroads on the time he wished to devote to instruction and supervision.   Accordingly, he resigned his
canonry in 1683.

Naturally his family protested when they heard of
his thus throwing away an office of so much distinction;   but they were not very much surprised.   They
had come to expect almost anything in the way of
self-denial from the saint when the interests of his
schools were at stake.   Besides, they remembered
that years before—prior to his ordination, in fact—
he had wished to resign from the canonry in order to
become a simple parish priest, and that he was **pre-**

vented from taking the step only by the refusal of his bishop to grant the necessary permission. Now that he had succeeded in getting rid of the honor, said his relatives, he would at least show some family feeling by naming his brother Louis, also a priest, to succeed him. But St. de la Salle did no such thing. He determined to allow no natural affection to guide him in the choice of a successor, and therefore nominated, not Louis de la Salle, but an obscure and devout priest who came of a humble family. The result was another storm of disapprobation from the saint's relatives; but the saint was getting used to storms.

And now St. John Baptist de la Salle was ready to take the final step in self-renunciation, to prove his generosity to God, to be in a position to say with the fisherman of Galilee, "Behold, we have left all things and have followed Thee."

As the eldest son of the de la Salle family, he had become, on the death of his father, a very wealthy man. Then as now, the possession of money confers distinction, and the citizens of Reims respected and honored the priest who had shown himself skilled in the management of financial affairs. His inheritance gave him an advantage in dealing with the world and in taking care of his teachers; he was able to secure them adequate shelter, and nourishing food, and proper nursing in sickness. But his money was a drawback, too.

For several months he had been impressing his followers, the teachers in the Christian schools, with the idea of giving themselves wholly to the splendid

work in which they were engaged. He pointed out
to them the desirability of their offering themselves
to conduct free schools as a society of Christian
teachers and of trusting to the goodness of God to
supply their temporal needs. But he found them slow
to respond to his appeal; and being a good judge of
human nature, he read in their eyes the doubts that
were clouding their minds.

The masters were saying to themselves that it was
all very well for their director to talk about depending
on the providence of God, for he had an abundance of
money to fall back on to relieve his own wants.
But with them it was another story. They were
poor men; they had no steady income, no rich
patrimony. Suppose they were to give themselves
entirely to the task of educating the poor boys of the
city and spend their youth and their talents in the
work; might not the schools be broken up, or might
not sickness come, or might not the weight of years
compel them to lay down the burden? What would
become of them then? He could afford to ignore the
future; but they could not.

St. de la Salle saw the force of these objections and
he met them squarely like the brave man he was. He
remembered that the great saints loved poverty as a
virtue especially dear to God; he recalled that his
Divine Master was so poor that He was born in a
stable and buried in a stranger's tomb; and so he
took the resolution of giving away all his wealth. He
would put' himself absolutely on a level with the
schoolmasters. They were poor men, dependent
solely on the goodness of God and the charity of the

faithful. Very well; he would make himself as poor and dependent as they. He would say with St. Peter, "Silver and gold have I none."

Once more he consulted the saintly Father Barré. Might it not be well to use his vast wealth to establish schools all over the land, to build suitable houses for his teachers to live in, to give them, by means of his money, the best possible training for their profession? But Father Barré, foolish, perhaps, as men judge of such things, but truly wise with the wisdom of God, thought otherwise. "If you found schools with your own money," he said, "they will founder. Build your educational work on confidence in God. By all means become poor, even as Christ was poor; but instead of putting your money into the schools, give it away in charity, to the needy and the afflicted. Be really generous, and God will take care of you."

St. de la Salle acted on this remarkable advice. Hard times came upon the land, sickness and famine stalked through the streets of Reims; and in that hour of dire distress the founder of the Brothers distributed every penny of his patrimony among the poor and the afflicted.

This great work of charity he conducted with as much method as is employed by the scientific organizations of our own day. The distribution was made with care and order. He began by seeing that the poor lads who attended the schools were properly fed. School luncheons were served regularly. Boys are boys the world over; for, we are told, the youngsters of Reims came to receive the food with much more eagerness than they came for instruction.

Then, every morning a breadline formed outside the house in New Street, a line not differing much from the breadlines that in time of stress form in our great cities to-day. There were honest workmen out of work, men who had lost their wealth through gambling and reckless speculation, professional beggars by the dozens, the halt and the feeble, the blind and the lame. They were all brought into the house and made comfortable, the saint himself or one of his assistants gave them a little talk about God or a short instruction on the truths of the Catholic faith, and then the hungry were fed and the needy relieved by presents of money. Sometimes he heard of people who, though they were poor and hungry, were ashamed to join the breadline. Such persons he found out and managed to help in such a way as not to wound their feelings.

His wealth was great, but the demands upon it were greater. One day the breadline stood at the door for a longer time than usual, for his money and provisions were all gone. Then the saint took a basket and went from door to door among the residences of the wealthier inhabitants, begging for food and money. In that way he was able to continue his good work until the period of famine was over.

St. de la Salle was now ready to found his Institute of the Brothers of the Christian Schools. He had made the supreme sacrifice. He had become a beggar for Christ's sake. And "God loveth a cheerful giver."

CHAPTER IX
THE TORCH-BEARERS

THE Feast of Our Lord's Ascension fell on May 10 in the year 1684. The date is worth remembering in this history, for it was on that day that St. de la Salle took the first steps toward organizing his school masters into a religious community. They were already teachers, and most of them good teachers. But they were to be something more. The saint was convinced that God wished them to be members of an organization, to be soldiers in an army of holiness and learning, to take upon themselves the obligations and reap the great rewards of men who lead what is called the religious life.

Great men do their great work in different ways, and they seek to have that work last after them; their work is, so to speak, their child, and it is their wish that it should continue in the world long after they themselves are dead. The great work of Shakespeare was his plays—glowing pictures of human life and soul-searching comments on men and things; and they remain in the world though he has been buried for more than three hundred years, and they are more cherished and admired to-day than when their author walked the London streets or sat beside the Avon. The great work of King Louis XIV was his kingdom, and in order to make it great and flourishing and, as he hoped, enduring, he fought many wars and braved many dangers and sacrificed the lives of thousands of his subjects. And his monarchy did last—for almost a century after his death.

St. de la Salle was neither a dramatist nor a king; but he had a great work to do—a work that truly was a greater work than the work done by Shakespeare or King Louis. That work was the spread of popular education, the bringing of learning into the minds of the people, the forming of boys and young men into upright Catholics and loyal citizens. And in order to make that work live after him, in order to bring the benefits of Christian education to generations yet unborn, he founded an institute, the Brothers of the Christian Schools.

In Greece in the days of her glory—the Greece of the poets and philosophers, the Greece of the victorious armies, the Greece of the Olympian games—there was a festival called the Feast of the Torches. The people would form in two long rows, extending mile upon mile, and down between the two lines of people relays of swift runners would speed along, one relieving the other, holding aloft a lighted torch. When one runner stopped exhausted, he would pass the flaming torch to another runner who would dash on down between the lines, and he in turn would hand on the torch to still another runner. The festival was not considered a success if the first runner, the man who had lighted the torch, let it fall to the ground or let it go out; that torch must be kept burning and kept moving all the time.

So it is with education. Learning is the light of the

human mind; were it to go out, the human race would be in darkness. And St. de la Salle, the man who kindled the torch of popular education in Reims, was not content to let the torch fall to the ground; he wanted to organize a little band of well-trained athletes who, passing the torch of learning from hand to hand, might carry it on and on, to city after city and country after country and generation after generation.

That is why, on the Feast of the Ascension, 1684, St. John Baptist de la Salle brought together the twelve leading teachers of his schools and spent seventeen days with them in council and in prayer. It was the first assembly of the Institute. They were to organize the torch-bearers, to discuss the means of making their educational work more fruitful and more lasting. The torch of Christian education was now alight; it was their business to keep it ever burning.

Much of their time during that retreat was spent in prayer. Like all the saints, the holy founder was a strong believer in prayer. He knew that he and his disciples could not act wisely unless they received light from Heaven. The rest of their time was taken up with the interchange of opinions regarding the organization of the teachers and the schools. In those discussions it was the schoolmasters who spoke first and the saint who spoke last; it was a thoroughly democratic assembly. Such a thing was very unusual in seventeenth century France, the France of Louis XIV; but in this, as in ever so many other things, St. de la Salle was far ahead of his times.

He realized that the best rules, the rules that are most likely to be respected and obeyed, are not the rules forced upon people against their will but the rules which people cheerfully impose upon themselves.

The masters were eager to bind themselves for life to the work of the schools; they wished to promise God to remain Christian Brothers for the rest of their days. The saint was pleased with their enthusiasm, but he knew so much about the inconstancy of human nature that he persuaded them to modify the plan. Instead, therefore, on the morning of Trinity Sunday, St. de la Salle and the first twelve Brothers knelt before the altar in the little chapel of the New Street house and made temporary vows— vows by which they promised to obey the superior of the Institute and to remain with the Brothers during one year. And as they made the promise, they held lighted candles in their hands—a happy symbol of the flaming torch of Christian education which they were to carry through the world.

It was at this first assembly, too, that the name of the Institute was adopted. Previously the teachers had been called masters. Henceforth they were to be known as Brothers—as the big brothers of the boys in the schools. The word *Schools* was included in the title of the Institute as a reminder to its members that its essential work is education—that they were not to be Trappists or Carmelites living apart from the world, but educators, in the world but not of it, giving their time and their talents to teaching. And the adjective *Christian* was added to show that in their work of teaching the Brothers were to imitate Our Lord Jesus Christ, the world's Supreme Teacher, and that in a special way they were to teach His holy doctrine. Such is the origin of the name, Brothers of the Christian Schools.

The following winter the Brothers definitely adopted the black habit, with the white collar, which they still wear. That collar, or rabat, as it is called, was much like the collar worn by priests in France in the days of Louis XIV. The habit itself differed from the priestly soutane by the absence of buttons—to this day the Brothers' habit is fastened with iron hooks—and by being worn without a belt or sash. Because he was a priest, St. de la Salle is represented in pictures as wearing the soutane and sash. He was the only priest who was ever a member of the Institute.

At first St. de la Salle thought of having priests in the Institute as well as Brothers, for in all the great orders of the day priests were considered necessary. He selected one of the most saintly and brilliant of the first Brothers, Brother Henry, and had him make his theological studies at the Sorbonne, in Paris. But, almost on the eve of being ordained a priest, Brother Henry took sick and died. It was a severe blow to the holy founder, who dearly loved this faithful disciple; but he accepted the occurrence as being an expression of the holy will of God. And the more he thought about it, the more he became convinced that there should be no priests in his Institute. The Brothers were to be teachers, they were to give their time and talents to school work, and for them the labors of the priesthood—like preaching and hearing confessions and attending the sick—though glorious works in themselves, would really be distractions from the great tasks of education to which they were devoting their lives. So he inserted in the rule of the Brothers the precept that they shall not become priests, nor even wear the surplice, nor perform any function in the church except to serve low Mass.

By means of this important rule, the founder of the Institute of the Christian Schools made clear the fact that the vocation to the Brotherhood is something distinct from the vocation to the priesthood. Even in our own time many persons fail to grasp the distinction. The Brothers are religious, making the usual vows and leading a community life; but they are not priests or students for the priesthood. In the strict sense of the word they are laymen, not clerics. Freed from the obligation of reciting the office, of answering sick calls, and of administering the sacraments, they are able to give their entire time to the three occupations to which they have devoted their lives: To prayer, for they are religious, wearing a religious habit and following a religious rule of life; to teaching, for that is the reason why their Institute came into existence, and it is impossible to think of the Christian Brother who is not a teacher; to study, for the man who ceases to be a student ceases to be an efficient teacher.

In founding the Brothers of the Christian Schools, St. de la Salle did something that had never been done before. True, there had been many religious orders in the Church before his time; but not an order of men devoted to teaching as the one essential work of their organization. Dominicans, Franciscans and Jesuits engage in teaching—indeed, those three orders have produced some of the finest teachers in the world; but they do many other things, like giving missions and visiting hospitals and prisons and acting as spiritual directors for men and women. But the Brothers of the Christian Schools are concerned with no external work but the education of boys and young men. As we shall soon see, St. de la Salle had no narrow conception of that work, and the Brothers of to-day who teach in colleges, not less than the Brothers who teach in orphan asylums, are working in harmony with the spirit of their founder; but the saint was insistent that nothing whatever—even so sacred a thing as the priesthood itself—should interfere with their work as teachers.

"All kinds of teaching, and nothing but teaching" —such might be considered the scope of the Brothers' external work as determined by St. de la Salle.

CHAPTER X
ON TO PARIS!

PARIS, the capital of France, is one of the four or five supremely famous cities in the world. If we were to cut from our books of history and literature and philosophy and science all that pertains to Paris, we should find very few pages left to read and think about. For centuries the kingdom of France was called "the Eldest Daughter of the Church," and the great city of Paris was the fairest jewel that blazed upon her brow.

Many and many a time in the world's history armies of invaders, seeking to conquer the French nation, raised as their battle-cry, "On to Paris!" "On to Paris!" cried the Burgundians, when they sought to wrest the sovereignty from the crabbed fingers of King Louis XI. "On to Paris!" cried the English under the gallant King Henry V when they triumphed over the French troops in the great battle of Agincourt. "On to Paris!" cried the Germans in 1870, when they inflicted a humiliating defeat on Napoleon III, and again in 1914 when they swept through Belgium and northern France, only to be checked at the River Marne.

And "On to Paris!" was the battle cry of St. John Baptist de la Salle. He was the leader of an army, and he sought to plant his banner on the walls of the historic capital of France. But the army he led was very different from the Burgundian army or the English army or the German army. His was an army of peace and love and goodness; a little army of educators who came, not to bring hatred and woe, but to spread knowledge and religion. His soldiers were the torch-bearers of Christian education, and the standard they carried was the cross of Christ. Of all the aspiring generals who at one time or another had cried, "On to Paris!" the founder of the Brothers was the first to march on the city with gifts in his hand and with love in his heart.

Like all men who do really great and good things in the world, St. de la Salle made his entry into the city very humbly and quietly. In February, 1688, accompanied by two Brothers, he arrived in the capital and undertook the management of a parish school. A pious priest, Father de la Barmondiere, had invited him, and the saint felt that the invitation came from God Himself, that it was God's will that the work of the Christian Schools, which had prospered so well in Reims, should now be carried on in the great city of Paris. And before very long God made it clear that it was indeed His holy will that the Brothers should spread the light of education in the French capital, for He blessed their work and made it possible for the saint to open several schools and to take many poor boys under his care.

Yet it was not easy work; God's work seldom is easy, for it is work that involves constant warfare against the powers of evil. You might think that a man coming to do nothing but good in the great city, a man who sought nothing for himself and who only

wanted to help needy boys get an education, woul
be received with open arms, that the people woul
gladly welcome him and help him in every way the
could. But such was not the case. The saints ir
all ages, the men who strove against sin and igno
rance, always had to fight hard, and St. de la Sall
was no exception to the rule. This great soldier o
Christian education eventually conquered the cit
and the country and the world; but first he had t
fight, and fight hard, against many foes who trie
to impede his efforts and destroy his work.

A long, hard battle the saint had to fight agains
envy and misunderstanding. When we study th
lives of great men, especially the lives of the saints
we find that the benefactors of humanity and th
servants of God are often annoyed and thwarte
by people who, while not really bad, nevertheless d
not understand and do not like to see others succee
in work in which they themselves have failed
Others had tried to establish schools in Paris an
had sought to control and educate the boys of th
Paris streets; and for various reasons they had no
succeeded in their attempts. So now, when St. de l
Salle, who was an educational genius, came alon
and taught the boys to like education and establishe
schools which proved successful, the men who ha
made the earlier attempts were envious of hi.
triumph and did all they could to hinder his wor
and even to force him and his Brothers to leave th
city.

Some of the opposition which St. de la Salle had
to face came in a way that is almost amusing. Many

of the boys who attended his schools in Paris used to work part of the time in a stocking factory. The men in charge of the factory liked to have the boys thus employed, for the lads did considerable work and received but very small wages for their labor. Before the Brothers opened their schools, the factory managers could call upon the boys to work for them at almost any time they chose, but St. de la Salle, who considered school-work more important than making stockings, insisted that the school hours should not be cut short at the whim of the hosiery manufacturers. The result was that the bosses protested and threatened, and even tried to make people believe that these new teachers were trying to destroy an important industry.

This difficulty St. de la Salle solved in an up-to-date and satisfactory manner. He saw that the poor boys needed an education, and needed it badly; but he also saw that they needed to continue their work of making stockings. What did he do? He sent to Reims for one of his Brothers who understood the hosiery industry and installed that Brother in the schools as an instructor in stocking-making. A portion of the school day was set apart for instruction in the trade, but the boys remained in the school and under the care of the Brothers while fitting themselves to take positions in the factory later on. This was the first of the trade or technical schools which the Brothers have since conducted in various parts of the world.

But soon another difficulty arose, a difficulty that would never have occurred if the schools of St.

de la Salle had not been such excellent schools. There were certain men in Paris known as the writing-masters, who managed to make a living by teaching boys to write. They were generally ignorant men, like the country schoolmasters of the day, but they were the only teachers to whom boys of the poorer classes could go for instruction. When St. de la Salle established his schools and offered absolutely free instruction, not only in writing but in other branches of study, it was natural that some boys who previously had been paying the writing-masters for tuition were glad to change to the new schools. And when the new schools proved so successful that they soon became the talk of the town, more and more of the pupils of the writing-masters came to the Brothers for instruction. The consequence was that the writing-masters, having fewer pupils than formerly, and therefore receiving less money, became very bitter against St. de la Salle and his teachers, whom they accused of preventing honest men from making a living and of taking the bread out of their mouths. They tried every means, even having recourse to lawsuits, to close St. de la Salle's schools and to drive the Brothers from the city.

St. de la Salle wished no harm to the writing-masters, and in founding his schools in Paris he had no thought of trying to put the writing-masters out of business. It was not his fault if the writing-masters' schools were so inferior that they could not stand a little wholesome competition. His purpose was to educate boys who were too poor to pay for

an education, and indeed most of his pupils were
boys so poor that the writing-masters would have
nothing to do with them. But, on the other hand,
the saint made it a rule not to turn away any boy,
rich or poor, who came to his schools. He suffered
keenly on account of the professional jealousy of
the secular teachers, but he remained steadfast in
his purpose of continuing his schools and of making
them and keeping them the best schools in the city.

His own Brothers, the masters whom he had
formed and guided and encouraged, whom he had
made into effective and successful teachers, were
not all as grateful as they should have been for the
careful professional training he had given them.
Some of them added to his troubles by severity with
their pupils, whom they foolishly sought to terrify
rather than to win by gentleness and devotion.
Some of them, seeing opportunities for themselves
and forgetting the ties of gratitude which should
have bound them to the Institute, left the organization and sought to establish schools of their own.
Some of them, whom St. de la Salle had placed in
positions of trust and authority, became too self-
important and independent—for power is always bad
for weak heads—and resented the kind and tactful
direction of the man who had made them. Some of
them were guilty of the disloyal and contemptible
error of not keeping their troubles at home and
insisted on making their complaints to outside
friends. Of course, in such cases the outside friends
—some of whom were envious of St. de la Salle
and his work—invariably sided with the discon-

tented Brothers, and agreed that the founder of the
Institute was unkind and incompetent.

Tongues wagged and wagged, as tongues are eve
prone to do, and the complaints of the few mal
contents lost nothing in the telling.   There ar
always to be found some good people who just can'
help telling bad news, and who are so anxious t
tell it that they generally don't wait to find out ho
true it may be.   Such persons were very numerou
in Paris in the days of Louis XIV, and the
succeeded in making such a stir over St. de la Salle
the Brothers and the schools, that on one occasio
the saint's ecclesiastical superiors, without investi
gation and solely on the strength of the evil rumors
ordered him deposed from the government of th
Institute and appointed a young priest to take hi
place.   The saint, with that humility and obedienc
which always distinguished him, promptly agreed t
step down from the head of the organization whic
he had founded and to which he had devoted th
best years of his life.   But with the Brothers it wa
another story.

The new superior was introduced to them, bu
they resolutely refused to accept him.   The majorit
of the Brothers had always been warmly attached to
St. de la Salle, and at this critical moment even most
of the discontented ones decided that a change could
only be a change for the worse.   The spokesman of
the Brothers respectfully but firmly insisted that
it was the determination of the teachers to have no
superior but St. de la Salle, that his direction was
necessary for the guidance of the Institute and for

the supervision of the schools; that, in short, were he deposed from office, the Brothers would give up the educational works in which they were engaged.

In the face of such a welcome the young priest who had been appointed to assume direction of the Institute promptly decided that the task was a little too strenuous for him. The matter was finally settled to the satisfaction of all concerned by having St. de la Salle restored to office.

CHAPTER XI
THE SCHOOLS OF THE PEOPLE

IN our country and in our day it is possible for
every child to secure at least the rudiments of an
education. Free grammar schools and high schools,
parochial schools and trade schools, are to be found
everywhere throughout the United States; and colleges and universities, maintained either by public
funds or by private endowment, are plentiful enough
to meet the needs of young people with the brains
and the energy necessary to secure the highest
scholastic training. We still have some men and
women in a few isolated parts of the country who
do not know how to read and write; but ordinarily
there is no excuse for such illiteracy. Certainly,
there is plenty of opportunity for learning.

Such was not the case in France in the age of the
Great King. There were colleges and academies for
the children of the nobility, though many members
of the French aristocracy declined to take advantage
of them. But for the common people there was a
notable dearth of educational facilities. We have
seen how poor was the teaching done by the secular
schoolmasters in city and country; but even if that
teaching had been of the very first order, the number
of schools was so small that only relatively few of
the children of the people could have enjoyed their
advantages. From time to time holy men and

women, realizing the importance of learning for the young, established schools for boys and for girls, but for the most part the efforts ended in failure. Not until St. de la Salle founded his Institute and opened schools for boys on an extensive scale, did the movement in favor of popular education take firm root and grow and prosper. Not until the graduates of his schools went out into the world and demonstrated the value of a sound, practical, Christian education, did the people begin to realize that scholastic training is something to be sought after and esteemed.

The boys who filled the first classes of the Brothers' schools in Paris were in many instances the sad products of the disorderly life that ebbed and flowed in the crooked streets of the great city. They were boys, some of them, whom their parents were unwilling or unable to control, boys with no feeling for discipline and piety, boys who had been running wild, and had formed undesirable habits of thinking and of acting. To change such lads into docile, studious, polite and devout pupils was not the work of a day. It was a task that required not only time, but much patience and a deep knowledge of human nature. In that almost impossible effort, St. de la Salle and his Brothers ultimately succeeded, but not until their nerves and their devotion had been sorely tried.

But a change—a change so great and so remarkable that all Paris noticed it—did come over the pupils of the Christian Schools. The boys who formerly had been ranging around the city in gangs, the terror of respectable citizens and the ready tools of rogues and scoundrels, now developed into well-mannered and self-respecting youths who entered and left their classrooms in order and silence, and who attended Mass with all the external marks of genuine devotion. They became interested in their books, and they attended instructions on Sundays as well as on school days.

How was the change accomplished? Certainly not by fear of punishment, for St. de la Salle insisted that flogging in any form must never take place in the schools of the Brothers. This rule he stressed in his recommendations to his teachers in words so strong and pointed as to leave no doubt of the disgust he felt for the practice of corporal punishment. But he had recourse to better and surer and more effective means. He made school life a pleasure instead of a task. He always acted like a gentleman himself, and the pupils were impelled, by admiration or by shame, to strive to imitate his own gentle and courteous manners. The importance of showing good example to the students at all times, of being models of politeness, was something which the holy founder never wearied of impressing on his Brothers. Most of his teachers learned the lesson, and the results were good order in class and the formation in the pupils of gentlemanly habits of speaking and acting.

But a still more important factor in the success of the schools established by St. de la Salle was his happy manner of making religion the center of educational life. Religion with him did not mean merely memorizing the catechism; it meant taking God into account in everything we do. The class exercises began and ended with prayer; and at frequent intervals during the school day a pupil would arise and reverently say aloud, "Let us remember that we are in the holy presence of God." Whereupon teacher and pupils would pause for a moment in their work and silently make a brief act of adoration. In every classroom there was a crucifix, and pictures of Our Lord, the Most Blessed Virgin and St. Joseph adorned the walls. The holy founder brought both teachers and pupils to realize that religion is the biggest thing in life, the most interesting thing in life, the most important thing in life, and that when they acted according to the dictates of religion they were doing something of benefit to themselves and something pleasing to God.

By means of instructions on the life of Our Lord and on the principal truths of the Catholic religion, the Brothers brought the boys to understand their faith and to love the practice of it. In the age of Louis XIV as in our own age and in every age, some people did not take religion seriously, did not make it a part of their lives. The purpose of the Christian schools was to bring the boys of Paris to see that a man who does not know and practice his faith is like a man who has lost the use of his limbs; he is helpless and cannot do what God wants him to do in the world.

St. de la Salle was successful in his work of educating the children of the people largely because he had the courage to break away from old-fashioned

methods of instruction and to suit the manner of
teaching to the times in which he lived. The founder
of the Brothers was full of new ideas and, even
though he was accused of being a radical, he was
brave enough to apply those ideas fearlessly to the
conditions which he faced and the problems which
he met. Like every educated man, St. de la Salle
had a great respect for the past, but he was clear-
minded and progressive and realized that many
things in the past were wrong, that many more
things, though good in their day, were no longer
salutary, and that even the best things that had
been accomplished in the past could be improved on
to suit the changing conditions of a new age. Let
us consider two instances of this wise progressiveness:
His adoption of the class method of teaching, and
his attitude toward the language of the country.

Until the time of St. John Baptist de la Salle,
what was known as the individual method of instruction was in vogue in the schools. Some earlier
educators had sought to improve upon it, and had
been in a measure successful; but it remained for
the founder of the Brothers to break away from it
entirely and to change, for good and all, the manner
of instructing children.

What was the individual method of instruction?
It was a method by which the pupils in the class
studied, usually in different books, and then recited
their lessons to the teacher one at a time. There was
no grading as we understand the term, no team
work, no studying of the same lesson by all the
pupils. The teacher gave his explanations and made

his corrections, not to all the pupils at one time, but to each pupil, one after another. One by one the boys would come up to the teacher's desk and receive their lessons; in the meantime the rest of the pupils could study by themselves, or just sit and dream, or even engage in some sort of play. The result was, of course, a great waste of time and a great deal of confusion. We have some old wood-cuts, dating from the sixteenth and seventeenth centuries, giving us views of the schools of the times. Most of them show that the pupils not directly under the eye of the master had what they considered a very good time; they were openly loafing or else engaged in what modern boys call "rough house." And even though in all the pictures the teacher is armed with a very businesslike-looking switch, it is clear that there was very little order in the schools.

All this St. de la Salle changed. He made it a rule that all the pupils should have the same books, that they should study the same lessons and that the instructions and explanations of the teacher should be given to all the pupils at one time. In the reading lesson, for example, while one pupil read aloud, all the other pupils were to follow him word by word in their books and be prepared to read aloud whenever called upon to do so by the teacher. If the reader made a mistake in pronunciation, the teacher, instead of making the correction himself, must call upon one of the pupils to point out the error. The pupils were carefully graded according to their proficiency, and silence was strictly observed in the class.

This method, known as the simultaneous or class method, is now in use in schools all over the world. It is so common and seems so natural that we are surprised to learn that any other method was ever used. Yet it was not until St. de la Salle adopted and perfected it in his schools in Reims and Paris that it had ever been successfully carried out. Not without reason has the founder of the Brothers been called the Father of Modern Pedagogy.

Again, for many centuries the language of learned men was Latin. It was known by educated persons all over Europe and was used exclusively by writers who wished their books to be read by the learned in Italy, France, Spain, and England. The languages of the various countries—languages like French or English or Portuguese—were called the common or "vulgar" languages; they were the languages of the people and many learned men looked upon them with something like contempt. This helps us to understand why Dante, the great Catholic poet of Italy, was criticized for writing his sublime poem, "The Divine Comedy," in Italian instead of in the learned Latin, and why scholars like Petrarch and Erasmus and Francis Bacon wrote in Latin the works which they considered their masterpieces.

But a change was coming over the world—indeed it had already come. The "vulgar" tongues, like Italian and English, were gradually but surely taking the place of the learned Latin. Dante had written in Italian, Vondel had written in Dutch, Shakespeare and Milton had written in English; and, right in the days of Louis XIV, Corneille,

Racine, and Moliere had written in French. The so-called "vulgar" tongues had become learned languages, and it no longer sufficed for a man to know Latin in order to be an educated man.

But, as is generally the case, the schools were behind the times. The little French boy going to even the elementary classes was taught to read and write, not his native tongue, but Latin; he was taught, not French grammar, but Latin grammar. This was not so bad for the sons of the aristocracy, who could stay at school for a long time; but it was very hard on the children of tradesmen and the poor who could look forward to only a few years of schooling. When leaving school they knew a little— usually a very little—Latin; and they knew no more French than if they had not gone to school at all.

St. de la Salle believed that the function of the school is to prepare the pupils for their after life; and in the after life of the boys in his Paris schools Latin was not going to play a large part. On the contrary, French was to be their language of conversation, their language of business, and the language in which were written the books they were most likely to read. So he boldly changed the whole scheme of education and insisted that in the schools of the Brothers everything should be taught in French. He maintained that a boy would make more rapid progress in his studies by learning in the language that he had begun to acquire in his babyhood, that he had heard in his home as a very little boy, that was used in the shops and in the streets and even in the sermons in church. And being a man who never did things by halves, and realizing that the time-honored practice of teaching in Latin could be banished only by employing the strongest possible means, he absolutely forbade the teaching of Latin in the Brothers' schools.

It need hardly be said that St. John de la Salle had no silly prejudice against the Latin language. He was a truly educated man and was therefore above prejudices. His own training had been a Latin training and he had a keen appreciation, not only of the beautiful Latin used by the Catholic Church in her official prayers and ceremonies, but also of the great secular Latin literature which was and is one of the glories of the world. But he was not only an educated man; he was a practical man. He knew that in his day there were schools where a boy could learn Latin if he wanted to learn it; but he realized the pressing need of having schools wherein would be imparted a thorough and practical knowledge of the language of the country. His schools were the schools of the people; it was right and proper that in them should be taught the language of the people.

CHAPTER XII
A GOODLY TREE

LET us reflect for a moment on the way a tree grows. It draws its sustenance from the soil, the air, and the sun, and slowly, but regularly and unceasingly, it increases in length and thickness and strength; it stretches out its branches and decks itself with foliage; and, if it is a fruit-bearing tree, it covers itself with pink or white blossoms, and when the blossoms fall the fruit begins to appear; slowly the fruit ripens, thanks to the warm sunlight, and presently you and I walk out into the orchard and pluck the fruit and taste it and say that it is delicious.

What is the most remarkable thing about the growth of the tree? It is that the tree grows from within. It lengthens its branches from the inside. It thickens its bulk from the inside. It produces its blossoms from the inside. The air helps it, the soil helps it, and the sunlight helps it; but it grows by itself, and always from the inside.

That is the way every living thing grows; that is why we speak of a growth from the inside as a vital growth. If a man were to go out into an orchard and pile some pieces of wood on the soil, and on top of the wood heap some flowers, and on top of the flowers place some apples or pears, nobody would think of saying that he was making a tree grow. That would not be a true growth, a vital growth, because it would not be a growth from the inside. And, similarly, if a small boy should stand on a box or pile books on his head, you would not say that he had grown; for really to grow, the boy must grow as the tree grows, from the inside.

The growth of an institution is in this respect like the growth of a tree or the growth of a boy; if it is to be genuine and vital, it must come from the inside. The tree grows because God has given it a something which we call a principle of growth; and a boy grows because God has given him, too, a principle of growth; and the Institute of the Christian Schools has grown because God gave it, through its learned and saintly founder, a principle of growth. That principle of growth, that something which has enabled it to increase and multiply and spread out from the inside, is called the spirit or soul of the Institute. If it had no spirit it could not grow, just as a boy's body could not grow if the soul were not in it. Now, what is the spirit of the Institute of the Christian Schools?

It is very easy to answer that question, because St. de la Salle himself has told us what it is in the rules he wrote for the guidance of his Brothers. It is a twofold spirit: The spirit of faith and the spirit of zeal.

The spirit of faith is a very real and very strong belief in God. The true Christian Brother always thinks of God first, always makes sure that he is doing what God wants him to do, always does his work—whether that work be prayer or study or teaching—because he is convinced that it is God's work. He reminds himself frequently that God is everywhere present, that God sees everything he does, that God knows everything that he thinks and desires and wills. St. de la Salle said that if a Brother has not this spirit of faith he should consider himself a dead member of the Institute, that he is like a branch broken off from the tree, a branch which will soon wither and die because it no longer shares in the growth of the tree.

The spirit of zeal, which is the second part of the soul of the Institute of the Christian Schools, is a spirit of interest, of energy, of enthusiasm for the Christian education of youth. Everybody is zealous or enthusiastic about something. The athlete is enthusiastic about the game he plays, the merchant is enthusiastic about his business, the artist is enthusiastic about his paintings, the priest is enthusiastic about preaching and hearing confessions and offering the Holy Sacrifice. And so the Christian Brother is supposed to be enthusiastic about the great work of teaching and the great work of study. If he lacks that interest, that enthusiasm, no matter how brilliant he may be and no matter how pious he may be, he has no business to be a Christian Brother; St. de la Salle sent away several candidates for the brotherhood who were both devout and learned, but who lacked this zeal, this enthusiasm, for teaching and study.

When we understand that faith in God and zeal for education constitute the spirit of the Institute, the principle of the Institute's vital growth, we are able to see just how it was that the schools established by St. de la Salle grew in number and spread all over France and ultimately reached out into all parts of the world. The Institute of the Christian Schools was like a tree. Its roots took hold of the soil in the city of Reims and its branches extended to Paris and to many other cities of France, and it has since brought forth blossoms and fruit in Italy, in Ireland, in Spain, in Canada, in the United States, in South America, in Asia, and in Africa. And just as, by means of grafting, a tree can be made to bear several different kinds of fruit, so the Brothers founded by St. de la Salle have conducted various kinds of schools.

It would not be especially profitable or interesting for us to learn all the details of the growth of the Institute in the time of its holy founder. City after city in France asked for the Brothers to open schools, and the saint, who was filled with faith and zeal, was very happy to accede to the requests. Much of his time he spent in long and tiresome journeys, making arrangements for opening new houses and superintending the work of his Brothers. He suffered much in many ways, but he had the great consolation of seeing the noble work to which he had devoted his life grow and prosper. He lived to see the little plant which he had so carefully watered and tended in Reims grow into a goodly tree with a stout trunk and with an abundance of foliage.

St. de la Salle began by opening free schools for the children of tradesmen and the poor, but that was not the only type of school to which he gave his attention. He was interested in every department of education, and whenever he saw the need for a particular kind of school he lost no time in supplying the need. His Brothers were the torch-bearers of Christian education, and he wanted them to bring the light of learning into any and every place shrouded in the darkness of ignorance. We have already seen how he early opened a trade school in Paris. It was not long before he established several other types of educational institutions in the capital and elsewhere.

One of the first of these new departures was the Sunday-school. He was not the first man to gather the children on Sundays for instruction in Christian Doctrine, for that practice had been followed by many illustrious saints before his time, notably by the great Cardinal-Archbishop of Milan, in Italy, St. Charles Borromeo. But the Sunday-schools established by St. de la Salle taught more than Christian Doctrine. They were intended mainly for young men who, working during the week, had no opportunity of getting lessons in the subjects they needed to learn. Such young men he invited to his schools on Sundays, and offered them several hours' instruction in reading, writing, literature, and mathematics. The session closed with an instruction on the truths of religion.

He also founded the equivalent of the modern high school, known as the Christian academy. Though he was first attracted to the field of elementary education, he saw the wisdom of giving a higher training to young men able to take advantage of it,

and accordingly opened classes offering advanced
courses in Franch literature, geometry, architecture,
mechanical drawing, and accounting. Some of those
subjects, prior to his time, had not been taught at all,
and he took pains to prepare some of the Brothers for
this novel and important work. The Christian
academy had two important results: It gave the
students a thorough training in several practical
subjects, subjects which would increase their earn-
ing power and efficiency; and it served to fill the gap
which heretofore had existed between the elementary
schools and the universities.

The first schools of St. de la Salle had been established to supply the educational needs of poor and
neglected boys and to help the children of tradesmen
in the cities of France. They were, as we have
seen, true schools of the people, the common people
who had had previously but slender opportunities
for securing an education. But the success of the
schools and the fine character of the young men who
were graduated from them soon attracted the attention of the wealthier classes and the nobility, and
early in the eighteenth century St. de la Salle was
asked to open a boarding college for the children of
the well-to-do. As usual, the saint lost no time in
acting on the suggestion. He had no narrow conception of the scope of his educational work. It was
not his intention to confine his Institute to but one
type of school or to supply the educational needs of
but one class of the people. It sufficed for him to see
the need for a school, any kind of school. His torch-
bearers were not to turn away from any opportunity

of forming character and imparting a Christian education.

There is a story of a lady in one of our modern American cities, who was alone in her house one quiet afternoon when she was startled to hear a noise in the dining-room downstairs. Timidly she investigated, and to her horror discovered a burglar filling a sack with her silverware. Almost out of her mind with terror, she crept cautiously down the front steps and rushed along the street looking for a policeman. At last she found one, and breathlessly told him of the intruder and begged him to come and make an arrest. But the policeman stroked his mustache and shook his head. "I can't help you, madam," he announced. "I am not on patrol duty; I am a member of the traffic squad."

Unfortunately, there are some educators who have as narrow a conception of their work as that police officer had of his. "It is not our duty to teach this or that type of school," they say; and they say it even when there is a pressing need for their services, when no other educators are there to take up the work. St. John Baptist de la Salle was not that kind of man. His faith in God and his zeal for learning were so great and so active that he was eager to take up any kind of needed educational work. That is why he established trade schools and high schools and Sunday-schools; and that is why he gladly opened boarding-colleges. And in order to make the boarding-colleges the best institutions of their kind, he made an exception in their case against his rule of charging absolutely nothing for the services performed by his Brothers. Obviously, there could be no such thing as a free boarding-college; so St. de la Salle sanctioned the practice of having the students in such institutions pay a specified sum for their maintenance.

Sometimes appeals for help came to him from country districts too small to maintain more than one teacher. In such cases he did not send a Brother, for he knew the dangers of living alone; but he took a number of secular men and taught them his methods of teaching, and then sent them into the country schools. This, the first normal school for secular teachers in the history of education, the saint conducted for many years at Reims and at Paris.

In another chapter St. de la Salle has been called an educational genius. Perhaps we are now able to see why. A genius is a man, specially gifted by God, who does some one thing supremely well, who is considerably ahead of his times, who discards old and time-worn methods, and invents ways of doing things that are practical and praiseworthy. Shakespeare was a dramatic genius, Napoleon was a military genius, Wagner was a musical genius. And St. John Baptist de la Salle was an educational genius.

CHAPTER XIII
THE IRISH BOYS

OVERLOOKING the Hudson River at Pocantico Hills, New York, not far from the Tarrytown and Sleepy Hollow made famous by Washington Irving in his "Sketch Book," is the novitiate and normal school of the Christian Brothers. The stained-glass windows in the beautiful chapel depict a number of scenes in the life of St. de la Salle and the history of his Institute. A visitor to the chapel is almost at once attracted to one of those windows in which a courtly gentleman wearing the insignia of a king is seen in converse with two churchly personages, one the Archbishop of Paris, the other St. John Baptist de la Salle. The courtly gentleman is none other than James II, King of England; and if the visitor knows something about English history and something about the character of the Stuart monarch, he will naturally wonder what King James is doing in a stained-glass window. Perhaps he will think of a certain episode in the Old Testament and smilingly ask: "What! Is Saul among the prophets?"

The story of that picture merits a prominent place in the history of St. de la Salle, for it helps us to understand the fine, broad views of education held by the holy founder as well as the high reputation as teachers the Brothers enjoyed before the close of the

97

seventeenth century. It opens up to us, likewise, an interesting phase of European history, and gives us a better insight into some of the international problems and conditions in the midst of which the Institute of the Brothers carried on its early work. So now let us take a glance at one of the most remarkable episodes in the history of the day, and find out how King James II managed to get into a stained-glass window.

After the death of Oliver Cromwell, the Lord Protector of England during the supremacy of the Puritans, Charles II, who had sought refuge at the court of Louis XIV after the execution of his father, Charles I, returned to England and was accepted as king. This event, known as the Restoration, occurred in 1660. When Charles II died, he was succeeded by his brother, the Duke of York, who ascended the throne under the name of James II. The new king was a Catholic; and although he was not in all respects a good man, at least he deserves credit for clinging to his faith in spite of opposition and for suffering persecution and exile because of that faith. There was a very strong feeling against Catholics in England and many of James's subjects disliked him and plotted against him. The opposition after a while grew so strong that offers were made to James's son-in-law, William, Prince of Orange, to come from Holland and claim the English throne. William and his wife, King James's daughter Mary, accepted the invitation, and James fled to France to secure from Louis XIV the aid of men and money to retain his place on the English throne.

The Great King received the deposed monarch

with lavish hospitality and gave him generous aid. He did so through policy as well as through kindness. France had become so strong as a military power that most of the other countries of Europe were leagued against her. Louis knew that if the Prince of Orange were successful in his attempt to win the English crown, England would be added to the league; whereas, if James were retained as king, England would be allied with France. Not long after, at the head of a French army, King James crossed over to Ireland, where many fighting men joined his ranks. William and his Orangemen hastily embarked for Ireland, and in July, 1690, the two armies met in the celebrated Battle of the Boyne. The result of that battle was a crushing defeat for the Irish and French, and James fled back to France. Several other attempts were made to reseat the unfortunate Stuart monarch, but all without success, and James II died in disappointment and exile in 1701.

Among those who had fought with James were many English and Irish nobles. When the cause seemed lost they followed the example of their sovereign and fled to France, where they were gladly welcomed at the court of Louis XIV. With them, in several instances, came their families, for Ireland was no place to live in for the families of the men who had fought against the Prince of Orange. The exiles, while planning other means of restoring James to the English throne, were installed with their monarch at St. Germain.

Among the exiles were some fifty Irish lads, totally

ignorant of the French language and of the customs
of the country on whose shores they had so suddenly
found themselves cast. Louis XIV desired to employ
them in various offices about the court, offices
befitting their talents and their rank in life, and so
sought for some means of educating them for the
posts they were destined to fill. The training of
the young strangers was a delicate and important
task, and the French king consulted the Archbishop
of Paris as to the teachers to be employed. The
archbishop considered the matter carefully and then
advised the king to entrust the Irish boys to the care
of St. de la Salle.

Were the founder of the Brothers less broad-
minded in his conception of the scope of his Institute,
he might have respectfully declined this work. He
might have pleaded that his schools were for the
poor, not for the nobility, that his work was for the
children of France and not for exiles from an alien
land. But the saint did nothing of the kind. He saw
in this offer simply another educational opportunity,
a chance for doing good, for molding youthful characters and for imparting learning to youthful minds.
Without the least hesitation he accepted the charge
and the fifty young Irishmen took up their abode in
one of his Paris boarding-schools.

A sad and homesick group of lads they must
have been at first, living in a strange land and learning in a strange tongue; but they were Irish and
therefore quick to adapt themselves to new conditions. Besides, St. de la Salle and his Brothers took
special pains to make the lot of the exiles as bearable

as possible, and concentrated on the task of imparting to them a sound and practical knowledge of the French language and of French history. One thing, at least, the exiles and their teachers had in common, and that was the Catholic faith. Before long this novel school was running smoothly and the Irish boys were making rapid progress in their studies.

Though King James had a good many troubles of his own, he did not forget the children of the men who had fought for him and for his rights. He was anxious to assure himself that they were happy and contented, that they were being well cared for and skillfully taught. So one day, accompanied by the Archbishop of Paris, the English monarch paid a visit to the school and greeted his little subjects. He was well pleased with things as he found them, and complimented St. de la Salle and his Brothers on the excellent results of the experiment.

That visit is the subject of the stained-glass picture in the novitiate chapel at Pocantico Hills. In the foreground, to the right, stands the king, copiously bewigged and beruffled, with his cane and his sword and his plumed hat, attended by a group of courtiers. In the center is the archbishop; and to the left, surrounded by his pupils, is St. de la Salle. In the background looms the teacher's desk with its books and pens; and on the wall hangs a large crucifix— a mute but impressive reminder to the exiled monarch that in that classroom the pupils learn to love and honor a King greater than earthly kings.

Of the subsequent careers of the lads who studied under St. John de la Salle in the exiles' boarding-school we know but little. Some of them doubtless remained at the court of Louis XIV and discharged satisfactorily the offices for which they were fitted. Some of them, we may be sure, took part in the several unsuccessful attempts to place the son and grandson of King James—known respectively as the Old Pretender and the Young Pretender—on the throne of England. More of them probably imitated the example of their fighting sires and in the French army struck stout blows against their English foes at Blenheim and Ramillies—and, maybe, even half a century later, at Fontenoy. The wanderlust, always so potent in Irish blood, may have lured others of them across the Atlantic to Canada and the southern colonies. All that is but a matter of conjecture. But it is pleasant to reflect that through them the influence of St. John Baptist de la Salle spread into divers professions and into various parts of the world, and that the young Jacobites were better and wiser men because of their contact with the holy founder.

And that is how James II of England happens to be in a stained-glass window.

CHAPTER XIV
THE MAKING OF A BROTHER

IN the course of the thirty-odd years during which St. John Baptist de la Salle devoted himself to the work of the Christian Schools, his society of religious educators had spread all over France. They had exercised their influence over the group of Irish youths, and a school had been established in the city of Rome, the capital of the Catholic world. The foundation of the Roman house is so interesting an episode in the history of the Institute of the Christian Schools, that a paragraph may profitably be given to it here.

Like all true Catholics, St. de la Salle loved and honored our Holy Father, the Pope, and he wished that his Brothers might establish a house of the Institute in the very city where the successors of St. Peter have ruled the Church. So he sent two of his disciples to open a free school in the Eternal City. One of the Brothers was taken sick on the journey and had to return to France; but the other, Brother Gabriel, went on alone, and took up his residence in Rome. He was very poor and he met with many difficulties, but at length he succeeded in starting his school and in keeping it open for thirty years. During all that time he was separated from the holy founder and the rest of the Brothers, but he was faithful to the charge entrusted to him by the saint and he persevered in his holy vocation and did much good for the poor children of Rome. He did not return to France until after the death of St. de la Salle. Ever since, the Brothers have maintained a house in the city by the Tiber.

So the Institute, in spite of envy and ignorance and opposition and persecution, had prospered. This it did, in the first place, because God blessed the work; in the second place, because the schools filled a manifest need; and in the third place, because St. John Baptist de la Salle exercised such great care in training his teachers and in supervising their classes. It is now time for us to consider just how that training was accomplished and to find out the ways in which the saint developed his Brothers in holiness and scholarship.

First at Reims, then at Vaugirard (now within the city of Paris), and then at St. Yon in Rouen, St. de la Salle maintained a central or mother-house of his Institute. Here candidates for the Brotherhood were received and trained and educated; here they returned in the vacations and at other times to renew themselves in piety and learning; and here they came to spend their days when sickness or old age impaired their efficiency in the classroom.

The saint, who had received his own vocation to the priesthood while still a boy, well knew that God often calls to His service willing souls in the first flush of their youth. Therefore, one of the departments of the mother-house was the Junior Novitiate, intended for boys who, while still too young and too unlearned to be teachers, nevertheless desired to take up educational work. These "little novices," as they were called, were the special objects of the saint's attention, and he labored to form them to habits of piety and to impart to them a relish for the things of the mind. They remained in the Junior Novitiate until they were sixteen or eighteen years of age. Then they entered the Novitiate proper.

Just as every army has its military academy or training-school, like the French St. Cyr or the English Aldershot or our own West Point, so every religious congregation has its Novitiate. It usually lasts one year. During that time the novices make sure of their vocation to the religious state, they strive to develop the virtues which should be practiced by men specially consecrated to God, they learn the particular rules and regulations of their institute and they study the obligations of the vows by which later they hope to bind themselves to the service of God.

The Novitiate of the Brothers in the days of St. de la Salle did not materially differ from the Novitiate of the Brothers in our own day. The candidates for the Brotherhood who are at this moment making their preliminary studies at Castleton, Ireland, or at Aurora, Canada, or at Pocantico Hills, New York, or at Ammendale, Maryland, or at Glencoe, Missouri, or at Martinez, California, follow substantially the same daily regulation that the saint's disciples followed at Vaugirard and St. Yon. The purpose of the Novitiate, then as now, was to lay the foundations of the religious life, and those foundations are the same at all times and in all places.

How do novices spend their time? Well, among other things, they sleep and eat and enjoy themselves like other human beings, but they do so at regular times and according to a prescribed rule. They learn the importance of regularity and of making the most of the time at their disposal. Thus, during meals, instead of chatting, they observe silence and listen to the reading of some good book; after repast they take a walk and discuss the book they have just heard read. Once a week they go for a long cross-country walk or engage in athletic sports, and every day they have an hour or so of healthful bodily exercise. Their studies during the Novitiate are entirely religious studies; they have a time for the reading of spiritual books, a time for the study of Christian Doctrine, a time for reciting vocal prayers, and a time for learning the theory and practice of mental prayer. They also have frequent exercise in the art of teaching catechism.

When the time of the Novitiate was over, St. de la Salle did not consider his young Brothers sufficiently prepared for teaching in the schools. He knew that to put a pious but ill-trained teacher into a classroom is often to do more harm than good, that the teacher who doesn't know how to teach is something like a square peg in a round hole—and sometimes like a bull in a china shop. The Father of Modern Pedagogy did not agree with those short-sighted, easy-going persons who tell us that "anybody can teach." He knew that teaching is an art and a profession, and that the teacher needs as much training, and perhaps more, than the doctor, the lawyer, the priest, the architect, or the expert accountant. He saw, as clearly as anybody, the great need of Christian schools; but he also saw that it was better to have no schools at all than to have them poorly taught and incompetently managed.

Accordingly, after completing the Novitiate, the young Brothers entered the normal training school. The Novitiate had laid the foundation of their religious life; the training-school was designed to lay the foundation of their educational life. In the training-school they did chiefly two things: They increased their own stock of learning, and they learned how to impart learning to others. Some of the first Brothers, odd as the attitude may seem, were rather afraid of learning; they fancied that to know very much would make them proud and ruin their piety. St. de la Salle was not long in showing them that scholarship, besides being a good thing in itself, was necessary for them in their lifework, that the teacher who has not a mighty love of books is like a soldier who dreads the conflict or a sailor who is afraid of seasickness. In the training-school the young teachers learned the principles upon which Christian scholarship is based.

One of those principles—a principle which we can all apply in our own studies—is this: The aim of every right thinking man is to grow more and more like unto God. Our Blessed Lord said: "Be ye perfect as your Heavenly Father is perfect." Now, God is infinitely perfect: He is not only Infinite Goodness; He is also Infinite Love, Infinite Beauty, Infinite Power, Infinite Knowledge. Pious persons

sometimes take a narrow view of God's Infinite
Perfection; they think only of His Infinite Goodness.
But the Catholic scholar, the Catholic man of learning, realizes that in proportion as he grows in knowledge—in proportion as he knows more of history and
philosophy and literature and science—he grows
more like unto God. Of course, what even the most
learned man knows is as nothing in comparison with
God's Infinite Knowledge, just as the holiness of
even the greatest saint is as nothing in comparison
with God's Infinite Goodness; but the fact remains
that both the scholar and the saint are more like to
God than the man who neglects improving his mind
and sanctifying his soul.

The young Brothers in St. de la Salle's normal
training-school also learned how to teach. They
received instructions in pedagogy, which is the art
of teaching, and those instructions were later embodied in a book written by St. de la Salle called,
"The Management of the Christian Schools." They
learned how to secure and maintain the attention of
their pupils; how to make their teaching interesting
and practical; how to conduct classes according to
the simultaneous method of teaching; how to give
their pupils a true taste for study; how to make an
impression on the hearts and the characters of boys.
They were made to give specimen lessons, and those
lessons were criticised by the Brother in charge of
the young teachers.

Even after they had completed the course in the
normal training school the young Brothers were not
considered entirely fitted for the work of the class-

room. They had the theory of teaching, just as a boy who has studied Spalding's "Baseball Guide" has the theory of our national sport; but they needed practice in the actual work of teaching, even as the boy needs practice in the actual game on the diamond. So usually St. de la Salle had his young teachers spend some time in the classes of experienced Brothers, observing how the theory of teaching was carried into practice, and how the details of the art of education were handled by men who understood their profession. Then they were given classes of their own.

Even then they were not left unaided and unguarded. The saint was persuaded that teaching is so important and so complex an art that it takes years and years to master it, and that every teacher now and then needs direction and advice. And, therefore, in the rules that he wrote for the guidance of his Brothers, he insists upon three distinct officials who are to supervise the work of the schools and the teachers. The first of these is the Brother Inspector, whose duty it is to observe the various teachers at work, to examine their pupils, and to report to the Brother Director of the community on the condition of the classes. The second is the Brother Director himself, who is to superintend the school, to guide and advise the teachers, and to call their attention to any defects he may notice in their educational efforts. The third is the Brother Visitor. This official is obliged to visit all the classes at regular intervals, to hold examinations in Christian Doctrine and the other subjects taught, to observe the conduct, not only of the regular teaching Brothers, but also of the Brother Inspector and the Brother Director, and to send a report of his investigations to the Brother Superior of the Institute. Never before was so elaborate a system of checks and balances applied to school work. It was a system thorough and complete, which shows how keenly the saint had studied every phase of teaching and school administration.

CHAPTER XV
THE ATHLETE OF GOD

THOUGH the idea may at first seem unusual to us, there is no novelty whatever in considering the saints as athletes. It was one of the most eminent of the saints, the great Apostle St. Paul, who compared the fervent Christian to the contender in the athletic games of Greece and who reminded us that the saint, like the athlete, must deny himself many things, must go through a course of rigorous training, must concentrate on his work, must diligently strive for mastery and must manifest both skill and endurance in the contest in order to win the prize. The athlete strives for a corruptible crown of laurel or parsley, the saint for an incorruptible crown of eternal glory. Let us in this chapter consider how St. John Baptist de la Salle showed himself to be a true athlete of God.

The boy who wishes to distinguish himself in school athletics must do several important things. He must, first of all, make up his mind to go out and win, to lower records, to know the game and play the game. Play the game he must, and play it hard. On a fine sunny afternoon, when he feels very much like sitting around and taking things easy, he must conquer the inclination and go out on the field and get dusty and heated and bruised; and he must keep up that daily practice right through the season.

And he must study the game—know it in its larger outlines and in its fine points. He must, too, observe experienced players in action and strive to learn the secrets of their success. And he must live a regular life, going to bed and getting up at fixed times, eating certain kinds of food and avoiding delicacies.

Our athlete of God, St. de la Salle, did all these things. The game he played was a more complex and exacting and interesting game than track work or football, but he followed the same general principles of training and practice. He was striving for spiritual perfection, for exceptional holiness of life; and while still very young, in a very real and vital sense, he was out to win. He was tremendously in earnest. He made holiness, sanctity, the absorbing interest of his life, and he bent every energy and all his will power to secure skill in the science of the saints.

Not for a single day did he neglect regular practice of his conflict with the enemies of salvation, the devil, the world, the flesh. These are the adversaries against which God's athletes fight a lifelong battle. He was careful not to expose himself to temptations, and when temptations came to him—when, so to say, his opponents broke through his line—he was quick to check the rush and recover his ground. And he was most exact in using the means of securing spiritual strength and agility, without which it is impossible to win in the game of holiness.

The means of becoming strong and active in the ways of God are chiefly two—prayer and mortification. All the saints were experts in prayer, for prayer is the food that nourishes the soul and strengthens the will to do good and avoid evil. St. John Baptist de la Salle was devoted to prayer. Not only did he recite the community prayers of his Brothers with reverence and attention, but he often prayed while going through the streets and on his long and frequent journeys all over France. He loved to recite the Divine Office, and when walking about he usually had his rosary beads in his hand. Even as a boy he liked to make frequent visits to Our Lord in the Blessed Sacrament. This liking increased with the years, so that if he was wanted at any time, he could almost always be found on his knees in the chapel.

The athletes of God give great attention to a certain kind of prayer that makes the soul grow in suppleness and strength. That form of prayer is what is called mental prayer or meditation. No matter how busy he might be with teaching or studying or superintending schools, St. de la Salle always spent several hours in mental prayer each day, and often he gave to this practice of devotion several hours of the night. As a young priest at Reims, every Friday he would spend the entire night in meditation in the church. Once a priest, who was staying at the Brothers' house, had occasion to go to the saint's room very late at night; he found the holy founder on his knees, intent on his conversation with God. Another time one of the Brothers found it necessary to go to St. de la Salle about four o'clock in the morning. He knocked several times at the door, and receiving no response, ventured to enter the room. The saint was lying on the floor beside an overturned prie-dieu; completely worn out by his toils and his vigils, he had fallen down exhausted in the midst of his prayers. He was like an athlete who overtaxes his strength and drops unconscious in the middle of the game.

The practice of mortification is an important part of the holy athlete's course of training. St. de la Salle, who knew how valuable this virtue is in laying the foundations of holiness of life, loved it and practiced it up to the hour of his death. As a boy and a young man he had been accustomed to the daintiest food, so when he first went to live with the Brothers the coarser food sometimes actually made him ill. He tried hard to overcome this delicacy of taste, and soon succeeded. One day the cook—who seems to have had the absent-mindedness that characterizes a good many other cooks—accidentally seasoned the food with wormwood. The Brothers had only to taste the dish to discover that a mistake had been made; but St. de la Salle paid no attention to the bitter taste, and continued to eat his portion. That is but one example out of many to show how he practiced exterior mortification.

He was not less adept in the mortification of his mind and heart. When he gave up his canonry and distributed his wealth among the poor, many persons told him to his face that he was a fool. Instead of getting angry or trying to defend himself, the saint would quietly agree with them and ask them to remember him in their charitable prayers. When he opened his first school in Paris some of the rougher elements among the people would hoot at him and pelt him with mud as he went through the streets. Such insults he endured patiently and even gladly, for they made him a little more like to Our Lord, who had been abused and mocked at as He carried His cross through the streets of Jerusalem.

In order to become more and more proficient in holiness of life, St. de la Salle studied the Lives of the Saints, that book which contains the history of God's most distinguished athletes. He there learned the details of the difficult art of sanctity, and encouraged himself to renewed efforts to grow more and more like to the martyrs and confessors of earlier days. Above all, he read daily in the New Testament, the wonderful book wherein Our Lord Himself has laid down the rules which His athletes are to observe if they would win the eternal crown of glory. He thought so much of this holy volume that he directed his Brothers to carry it about with them always and to read a portion of it every day. For he wanted his Brothers to be God's athletes, too. They were to be the torch-bearers of Christian learning, and it was in the New Testament that they were to find the source of light and strength.

A mark of the boy athlete is that he is always loyal to his school. He tries to win games, not merely for his own personal glory, but for the honor of the institution he represents; that is why he wears the school's monogram on his running suit or the block letter on his jersey. Similarly, St. de la Salle was characterized by intense loyalty to our Holy Mother, the Church. He had the deepest reverence and love for the Pope, and he honored and obeyed the bishops as the successors of the Apostles and the representatives of God. This loyalty of his was severely tested owing to the fact that in the days of Louis XIV in France some Catholics took part in a movement which was condemned by the Church. That movement is known as Jansenism.

The Jansenists were people who had wrong ideas about grace and free will, and who in their conduct aimed at being extremely strict and rigorous. They thought, for example, that only very great saints should receive Holy Communion often, and they made the business of saving one's soul much harder than it really is. They were something like the Pharisees in the time of Our Lord and like the Puritans in seventeenth century England. Indeed, we can understand this matter fairly well if we try to remember that the Pharisees were long-faced Jews, the Puritans were long-faced Protestants, and the Jansenists were long-faced Catholics.

Although he was a very holy man who could, when necessary, be very severe with himself, St. de la Salle was in no sense a long-faced man. He accounted good humor one of the marks of true devotion. His own habitual expression was gentle and pleasant; and he distinctly tells his Brothers in the rules he composed for their guidance to endeavor to have a cheerful rather than a melancholy countenance. Once he noticed a Brother who was looking somewhat surly and sour, and the holy founder said quietly, "My dear Brother, try not to go around with a face like the door of a jail."

Nor did he possess those habits of mind of which a long face is the outward indication. He had no sympathy with the gloomy doctrines of the Jansenists, who looked upon God as a sort of tyrant, eager to punish us for all our weaknesses; to him God was a kind and loving Father, who should be served through love rather than through fear. Some very learned and pious men of the time—including the brilliant writer, Pascal—and even some priests and bishops, were Jansenists; but St. de la Salle was on his guard against their errors and took every precaution that his disciples might not be led astray. Some of the Jansenists tried hard to win the saint over to their party, and offered to finance a novitiate for him and to endow several schools; but he would have absolutely nothing to do with them. When the sect was formally condemned by the Pope, St. de la Salle publicly announced his obedience to the Holy Father; and in his last words of advice to his Brothers he urged them to keep ever faithful to the teachings of the Church. Such was the loyalty of a true athlete of Christ.

As the well-rounded athlete excels in many forms of sport, so St. de la Salle carried all the virtues to a high degree of perfection. His active faith, his ardent love of God, his self-sacrificing devotion to the welfare of his neighbor, his deep humility, his spotless purity, and his desire to do in all things the holy will of God, were the admiration of all who, knew him. Every practice of Catholic piety was dear to his heart. He loved the Mother of God with a tender, filial devotion, and always spoke of her as the

Most Blessed Virgin, a beautiful custom which is to this day perpetuated by the Brothers and their pupils. He placed his Institute under the protection of St. Joseph, and he urged his Brothers to encourage their students to have a special devotion to the Holy Guardian Angels. A saint to whom he was particularly attached was like himself a teacher-saint, St. Cassian or Cassianus, who is one of the characters in Cardinal Wiseman's novel, "Fabiola."

When we read of the many schools founded by St. de la Salle, of the success with which he formed his teachers, of the numerous improvements which he introduced in educational work, of the great good he performed in the world, we may well wonder how he managed to do so much and to do it so thoroughly and well. The secret of his success is his holiness of life. The roots of the tree he planted and made to grow so tall and straight were his Christian virtues. He was able to work manfully for the Church and for the state, for the salvation of souls and for the spread of learning, because he was a superb athlete of God.

CHAPTER XVI
PICTURES IN LITTLE

The Saint's Personal Appearance

ST. JOHN BAPTIST DE LA SALLE was a man somewhat above the middle height, with lofty forehead and bright blue eyes. His complexion, fair in his youth, had become almost swarthy in consequence of his exposure to all kinds of weather in the course of his long and frequent journeys on foot through all parts of France. His abundant brown hair had turned prematurely white. His nose was long and regular; his mouth well shaped, the lips full and slightly prominent and habitually shaped into a kindly smile. His bearing was at once dignified and graceful. His health had been delicate in his youth, but his regular life and his force of will contributed to give him a vigorous constitution. During his last years he suffered intensely from a sore on his knee on which some of the ablest surgeons of Paris and Rouen exercised their skill in vain.

Sometimes we get the notion that the saints in daily life resembled the saints we see depicted in stained-glass windows and in idealized holy pictures. We think of them as men who always had the whites of their eyes turned upward and who had faces that absolutely could not ripple into smiles. This impression is very misleading, notably so in the case of the founder of the Brothers of the Christian Schools. Everything in the personal appearance of St. de la Salle was gentle and peaceful, because his soul was always in union with God; but everything was likewise winning and attractive. He had the alertness and vigor of the true teacher, and the personal magnetism always found in leaders of men. He inspired love, not fear; and both Brothers and boys were always glad to go to him with their doubts and troubles and difficulties.

His Rules of Life

Earnest and thoughtful men, especially the saints, have often drawn up rules for their own guidance, rules which enable them to utilize their time and perform their duties to God and man with thoroughness and care. This practice was followed by St. John Baptist de la Salle, and the rules which he drew up for his own direction afford us an opportunity of learning much about his attention to daily duties and about the spirit of faith which animated all his actions. Here are some of them:

"I will daily spend a quarter of an hour in renewing my consecration to the Most Holy Trinity.

"I must be convinced that in performing faithfully the duties of my state in life I am most surely pleasing God and securing my own salvation.

"When visiting any one I will be careful to speak only of what is necessary and not engage in mere worldly gossip.

"During the day I will at least twenty times unite

my actions with those of Our Blessed Lord, and I will try to share His views and intentions in performing them.

"When the Brothers come to me for advice, I will ask Our Blessed Lord to speak to them through me.

"Should anybody cause me pain, I will be careful to keep silence.

"I must be careful not to lose time; great watchfulness alone will help me in this matter.

"It is a good rule to be less solicitous to know what we are to do than to do perfectly what we know should be done.

"In the morning I will take a quarter of an hour to plan the work of the day and to foresee my possible failures in order to prevent them.

"I must not pass a single day without visiting the Most Blessed Sacrament. When traveling, I will make it a point to visit the church in every village through which I may pass."

The Bishop's Cloak

Loving poverty, a virtue especially dear to Our Lord, St. de la Salle, though always scrupulously clean and neat, habitually wore clothes that gave evidence of age and usage. One cold day, when he had been asked to dinner by a certain bishop, the cloak he wore was so thin that the prelate insisted on his accepting a new warm one. The saint preferred to keep the old cloak, but he was too much of a gentleman and too much of a saint to refuse a present from his ecclesiastical superior. Shortly afterward, however, while he was wearing the bishop's gift, he was attacked by two robbers who took the cloak away from him. The saint was inwardly delighted that he was thus given an opportunity of practising poverty, and his only comment on the episode was the exclamation that in good fortune and in bad fortune invariably fell from his lips: "God be blessed!"

On another occasion he was again attacked by robbers who proceeded to divest him of his cloak and soutane. But when they saw how thin and poor his clothing was, they had not the heart to take anything from him and allowed him to go peacefully on his way.

In the Snow Ravine

On one of his journeys, shortly after he had organized his teachers at Reims, St. de la Salle lost his way in a blinding snowstorm. In his efforts to find the road, he fell into a deep ravine of snow, and there, stunned and almost frozen to death, he lay during most of the night. Time and time again he tried to climb out of the ravine, but the loose snow gave him no foothold and he always slid back to the bottom of the ditch. Finally, he offered a fervent prayer for God's assistance, and then, making one more effort, he succeeded in clambering to the brink of the ravine and in locating the country road. As he proceeded on his way he earnestly gave thanks to God for this almost miraculous rescue.

The Priest in the Bastile

We have all heard stories of the Bastile, that grim prison where men were often confined on mere suspicion and where the dungeons were cold and dark and gloomy. It happened that one day a message came from the Bastile to St. de la Salle. One of the prisoners, an unfortunate priest, asked him to come and hear his confession. The saint gladly consented; and the sight of the prisoner drew tears from his eyes. The poor priest had been totally neglected for several years. He was half starved, his soutane was falling into shreds, his undergarments were torn and filthy and he was covered from head to foot with vermin. The cell was disgustingly dirty and ill-smelling. St. de la Salle warmly embraced the abject prisoner, after which he heard his confession, listened to the story of his sorrow and offered him all the consolation he could. As he was leaving, an heroic idea suddenly occurred to him.

"Here," he said to the prisoner, "you take my clothes and give me yours."

The poor prisoner could hardly believe his ears, but St. de la Salle persisted in making the exchange; and a few minutes later he walked smiling out of the Bastile, gladly wearing the prisoner's filthy and ragged clothes. A great joy filled his heart; and we may be sure that the words of Our Lord sang themselves in his memory: "I was in prison and you visited Me, I was naked and you covered Me."

"The Wisdom of the Fool"

Early in the history of the Institute, St. de la Salle succeeded in interesting the Duke of Mazarin in the work of establishing free schools. One day the saint and the duke called upon a bishop to secure permission to open schools in the diocese. They pleaded their cause with much eloquence, but they failed to make much of an impression on the prelate.

"Nonsense!" exclaimed the bishop. "You are two fools."

"Oh, no, your Lordship," said St. de la Salle gently. "Only one"

The Saint and the Scotchman

Although St. de la Salle prayed much and thought much while traveling, he was invariably courteous and companionable in his attitude toward his fellow-travelers. One day on the road to Soissons he fell in with a young man, a native of Scotland, who intended to make his fortune in Paris. They had great difficulty in conversing at first, for the saint could not speak English and the stranger had only a slight knowledge of French. The Scotchman understood a little Latin, however; and so, speaking in a strange jumble of three languages, the two travelers managed to exchange ideas. The saint learned that the young man was a Calvinist who had been brought up in the midst of strong anti-Catholic prejudices and who had the most horrible and ridiculous notions about confession and other doctrines of the Catholic Church.

St. de la Salle had a great zeal for the salvation of souls, so he determined to enlighten the mind and soften the heart of this well-meaning but misguided exile. He paid all the young man's expenses on the journey, for the stranger had very little money, and when they came to a city where the Brothers had a house, he took his new-found friend with him and lodged him comfortably. They had daily conversations together, the saint answering the Scotchman's questions about the Church and explaining to him the essentials of Catholic teaching. The stranger was very obstinate in his opinions, but gradually his reason was convinced of the falseness of his position, and after some three months he eagerly sought to be received into the Catholic Church. He became a fervent and intelligent Catholic; and having returned to Scotland, not only persevered in the true faith, but succeeded in bringing into the Catholic Church all the members of his family and a number of his neighbors. All those conversions were made possible by reason of St. de la Salle's kindness and charity.

The Bogus Priest

On another of his journeys St. de la Salle fell into conversation with a man dressed like a priest who, before the day was over, confessed to the saint that he was really no priest at all, but a degraded criminal who had been guilty of the most dreadful sins. He had been so hardened in evil-doing that he had even presumed to handle the sacred vessels and pretend to say Mass. The winning personality of the saint was the means chosen by God to bring this unfortunate creature to realize the depth of his depravity, and the sweet and earnest eloquence of the founder of the Brothers persuaded him to repent of his sins and resolve to change his manner of life.

The saint brought him to Paris and invited him to live at the Brothers' house. Shortly after, St. de la Salle found it necessary to leave the metropolis for a while, and on his return he found a state of affairs bordering on the ludicrous. The news having leaked out that the guest was a clever and dangerous criminal, the Brother Director became alarmed at having so notorious a person in the establishment, and took strenuous measures to keep him from doing mischief. He gave orders that the stranger should be locked up and carefully watched and guarded; and the entire community was very uneasy until the saint returned and quieted their fears.

Then St. de la Salle resumed his care of the unhappy soul. The criminal made a general confession and was restored to the bosom of the Church. Even then the friendship of the saint did not end, for he used his influence to secure employment for his convert.

In Time of Need

During the first years at Paris the most unhappy man in the Brothers' house was the Brother who had charge of the kitchen and dining-room, for often the community was so poor that it was impossible to tell where the next meal was coming from. The poor Brother, without provisions and without money, would go and tell his troubles to St. de la Salle. The saint would counsel him to have patience and trust in God; and then, somehow or other, often by what looked like a miracle, there would come a present of food or money sufficient to tide the community over the difficulty. This happened so often that in time the Brothers became used to it—except the Brother who had to do the buying and the worrying.

On one such occasion, with not a penny in the house and with not enough food for the next meal, the Brother in charge ventured to go to the superior of a religious order near by and ask for a little assistance. The superior received him coldly, told him that the Brothers had no sense in trying to support a community without adequate financial means, and that the best thing for them to do was to get out of Paris; for his part, he would give them no assistance whatever. Very downhearted, the poor Brother started back home. On the way he picked up a package of papers which he brought to St. de la Salle to examine.

'God be blessed!" exclaimed the saint. "It looks as though God wants our neighbors to assist us, after all."

The papers proved to be some valuable documents belonging to the religious order whose superior had been so harsh and uncharitable. The Brother retraced his steps, this time bringing the papers, and the superior now received him kindly, thanked him for restoring the package and immediately sent a generous donation of food to the Brothers' house.

CHAPTER XVII

THE GATEWAY TO LIFE

WHENEVER an election is held in one of our American cities the candidates for the various offices make many speeches and write endless articles in the newspapers, all telling the dear public the wonderful things they will do if the people have the good sense and the good taste to elect them. The candidates make it very plain that they want the offices, that they are ready to do almost anything in order to be elected. The professional politician doubtless has virtues of his own, but modesty is not one of them. His favorite flower is not the blushing violet.

The saint is in this respect utterly the reverse of the politician. The saint does not put himself forward. He does not seek posts of honor and responsibility. He fears positions of power and trust, for he knows so much about human nature, in himself and in others, that he dreads the very real dangers inherent in the exercise of authority. He heartily agrees with one of the kings in Shakespeare's plays that, "uneasy lies the head that wears a crown."

Several times during the course of his life, St. de la Salle had tried to relieve himself of the responsibility of being the superior of the Institute of the Christian Schools. But he was so successful in guiding the teachers and in conducting the schools

128

that his Brothers felt that nobody could take his place. In 1717, however, when once more he pleaded to abandon the office, the Brothers reluctantly acceded to his desire. He was now an old man, his arduous life had told on his health, he was suffering most of the time from the sore on his knee and from severe attacks of rheumatism. He felt that he had not much longer to live, and he wanted to spend his declining days in preparation for death. Besides, it was time that the Institute he had established should, so to say, learn to stand on its own feet, that the Brothers themselves might conduct its affairs, and carry on the work of the schools without the aid of the experienced man who had already done so much for them.

All these motives impelled the Brothers to accept the resignation of the holy founder and to elect one of their number, Brother Bartholomew, in his place. This event occurred at the second general chapter of the Brothers, held in Rouen in 1717. It was the second conclave of the torch-bearers; and the bright and unfailing guiding torch, which the saint had held aloft for nearly forty years, was passed into other hands. Brother Bartholomew was one of the dearest friends of the saint, and one of the most fervent and self-sacrificing of the Brothers.

Freed from the cares of office and the numerous distractions and annoyances incidental to it, St. John Baptist de la Salle turned all his attention to prayer and meditation, and to revising the books he had written for the Brothers and their pupils. He was not a writer in the sense that he had devoted any considerable part of his life to the composition of books; but he had found it necessary to write several volumes bearing on the life led by the Brothers and on the work of the schools. This is a good time to consider his written work.

First of all were the Rules or Constitution of the Brothers. Every religious congregation has its rules, that is, the laws and directions furnished the members for their guidance. No organization can exist without rules. That is why we must have rules for a debating society, rules for playing baseball, rules for conducting a school. The Rules of the Brothers were written by St. de la Salle after much reflection and much prayer and after numerous consultations with his disciples. All the rules had been carefully tried in practice before being set down in writing; and now, after years of experiment, they were embodied in permanent form.

Besides the Rules, St. de la Salle wrote a number of meditations on the Sunday Gospels, in which he applied Our Lord's teachings to the school and community life of the Brothers, and also a book called, "Explanation of the Method of Mental Prayer." We have seen how highly the saint esteemed the practice of mental prayer. In his book he tries to make meditation easy and fruitful for his disciples; and he shows not only his deep piety but his remarkable knowledge of what to-day is called psychology, that is, the workings of the human mind. Other writings of the saint, dealing with various aspects of the religious life, are gathered together in a book called, "Collection of Short Treatises."

All the books just mentioned are concerned chiefly with the religious side of the life of the Brothers. On the educational side he wrote a book which has been the admiration of educators for more than two centuries, a book to which the English writer, Matthew Arnold—whose father was the eminent Dr. Arnold of Rugby—has paid a glowing tribute. That book is "The Management of the Christian Schools." In it the saint outlined his simultaneous method of teaching, and set down a large number of practical hints for maintaining discipline and for teaching the several school subjects.

For the pupils of the Brothers, St. de la Salle wrote several little works, including a set of "Rules of Politeness." The saint always maintained that the schools of the Brothers should be schools of good manners, and in this volume he brings together a number of precepts concerning daily actions which will help young men to form gentlemanly habits. In it he urges them to seek to imitate Our Lord, Who was the world's perfect Gentleman. He also wrote a book on Christian Doctrine called, "The Duties of a Christian." In an interesting and agreeable style he discusses the sacraments and the commandments and the virtues which Catholics ought to practice.

In 1719 the illness of St. de la Salle increased. He developed an acute case of asthma, and he suffered much from an abscess in the head. Far from complaining, he accepted his pains joyfully, reminding himself of what Our Lord had suffered on the cross and rejoicing in sharing his Saviour's heavy burden. When the doctor told him that he had but a short time to live, the saint calmly said: "I hope that I shall soon be delivered out of Egypt, and be admitted into the true Land of Promise."

That is the way with all the saints. They were glad to die. And why? Because death was no death for them. Worldly people find the thought of death a disagreeable thought; they try to banish it from their minds. But the saints like to dwell on the thought of death, for to them death is not the end of everything, but the beginning of everything. The day of their death is their real birthday. To them death is the gateway to life.

On the feast of St. Joseph, one of the patrons of the Institute, St. de la Salle, who had been for many days confined to his bed, was able to arise and offer the holy sacrifice of the Mass—a consolation which he highly prized. But a relapse came almost immediately. In Holy Week he was so ill that the Holy Viaticum was brought to him. In order to welcome his Lord with every outward mark of respect and devotion, the saint had himself dressed in soutane and surplice, and he received the Holy Communion kneeling on the floor of his room.

That was on Wednesday in Holy Week, April 5. The following day, Holy Thursday, he received the sacrament of Extreme Unction. On Holy Thursday evening the Brothers gathered about his bed, and the new superior, Brother Bartholomew, begged the dying saint to give them a last word of counsel and advice. The holy founder spoke briefly, urging them to be faithful to their holy vocation, and to avoid the evil influence of the world. A little later they all said together the beautiful hymn which begins the Brothers' evening prayer, "*Maria, mater gratiæ*," "Mary, Mother of Grace, sweet Mother of Mercy."

It was an impressive moment. Here were the faithful disciples, the men who had vowed their lives to the glory of God and the education of youth, kneeling about the bed of the man who had guided them in their lives and in their work. He was their Father in God, their model and their inspiration. And though tears of honorable human grief filled their eyes and choked their voices, they did not sorrow as those who have no hope. For the spirit of faith, the soul of their Institute, told them that death was coming to their saintly founder as a crown of glory and a surpassing great reward, that he was entering the portals of heavenly happiness, that in his case truly death was the gateway to life.

A little later, in response to a question put by Brother Bartholomew, the saint uttered the last words he ever spoke this side of the eternal gateway. Those words were: "I adore in all things the will of God in my regard." Such were the sentiments that had guided him through all the labors and trials of his well-filled life.

At four o'clock in the morning, the saint's face suddenly brightened and his habitual smile glowed upon his countenance. He looked fixedly and joyously for a moment into space, made an attempt to rise, joined his hands and lifted his eyes to heaven. In that posture he calmly breathed his last. It was Good Friday, April 7, 1719.

The news of his death spread quickly through Rouen and through France, and the words that came spontaneously to thousands of lips were these: "The saint is dead! The saint is dead!" Members of the aristocracy jostled with tradesmen and beggars in order to be present at his funeral; and as his body was borne through the streets of Rouen on the shoulders of his Brothers, the prayers and tears of the people whom he had so deeply benefited and for whose education he had so valiantly labored followed after like a cloud of incense. His remains, first interred at Rouen, now repose in the mother house of the Institute at Lembecq-lez-Hal, in Belgium.

St. John Baptist de la Salle was canonized by Pope Leo XIII in 1900, and his feast day, May 15, is observed throughout the entire Catholic world. In the formal decree of canonization, the illustrious pontiff uttered a sentiment with which this little story of St. John Baptist de la Salle may most fittingly close:

"Benediction, glory, and thanksgiving to Jesus Christ, God and Redeemer of the human race, who hath clothed His faithful servant, John Baptist de la Salle, with the splendor of His glory, and who, knowing our needs, has proposed him to us as a model, in order that we may the better know the supereminent charity of Jesus Christ which surpasses all knowledge, and be filled unto the fulness of God."

THE PRAYER OF THE CHURCH

Each year, on the fifteenth of May, the Catholic Church keeps the feast day of St. John Baptist de la Salle, and during the Mass, priests everywhere throughout the world read the following beautiful prayer:

"O God, who didst raise up St. John Baptist, Confessor, to give a Christian education to the needy, to guide young men in the pathway of truth and to form anew a family in Thy Church, graciously grant unto us that through his prayers and example we may be fervent in zeal for Thy glory in saving souls and grow worthy to share his crown in heaven."